94

54

74

42

84

12

60

Making Every Day Delicious

The recipes in this family-friendly collection are as easy to prepare as they are flavourful. As always, we have developed these recipes to reflect the latest culinary trends and have worked to ensure that the ingredients for most are readily available in communities across Alberta.

The ATCO Blue Flame Kitchen trademark is your assurance that each recipe has been tested in our professional kitchens and meets the highest standards.

There is more to our story than cookbooks and recipes. ATCO Blue Flame Kitchen has been providing household advice and tips on energy safety, conservation and efficiency for more than 85 years. The service has been expanded to include cooking classes and educational programs for participants of all ages.

Now, there are more ways to connect with us than ever before. For recipes, household tips, and expert advice, visit us online at www.atcoblueflamekitchen.com. To connect directly with a Community Educator-Professional Home Economist, reach us by email at bfkanswerline@atcogas.com, chat live with us via our website and app or call our toll-free line at 1.877.420.9090.

With families increasingly turning to the Internet for culinary tutorials and household advice, we've dedicated ourselves to serving this community online. Bring technology into your kitchen with our app that contains more than 3000 tested recipes and follow our regular tips on Pinterest, Twitter, YouTube, and Facebook.

If you've never been to an ATCO Blue Flame Kitchen cooking class, consider giving one a try. Classes are now available in Calgary and Edmonton – the food is great and topics vary widely. All of our class calendars are posted on our website, along with registration information.

Enjoy!

From the ATCO Blue Flame Kitchen team

10035 - 105 Street, Edmonton, Alberta T5J 2V6
909 - 11 Avenue SW, Calgary, Alberta T2R 1L8

To contact the ATCO Blue Flame Kitchen Answer Line
from the Edmonton area, call 780.420.1010;
from Lloydminster, call toll-free 1.306.825.5010;
from other locations in Alberta, call toll-free
1.877.420.9090.

Email: bfkanswerline@atcogas.com
Visit: atcoblueflamekitchen.com
Live chat available online.

Printed and bound in Canada.

Nutritional analysis completed by Revive Wellness Inc.

Bringing Technology to the Kitchen

Cooking at home has never been easier thanks to ATCO Blue Flame Kitchen's convenient, interactive digital tools for the family chef.

Download our FREE ATCO BFK App today!

 Chat live with our team of Community Educators and Professional Home Economists about recipes, food safety, stain removal and other household problems.

Need tips on cooking, recipes, food safety, stain removal and other household problems? We can help.

Our team can answer questions like these year-round:

What temperature should my fridge and freezer be set at?

Can I barbecue a turkey?

I left groceries in my car overnight. Can they still be eaten?

I'm hosting a party. Can you suggest some recipes?

How long can I keep condiments in the fridge once they are opened?

Email: bfkanswerline@atcogas.com
Visit: atcoblueflamekitchen.com
Call: 1.877.420.9090

Tips for success with ATCO Blue Flame Kitchen recipes

- Assemble the ingredients and prepare them as directed in the ingredient list before proceeding to the method.

- Measure liquids in glass or clear plastic liquid measuring cups. Measure dry ingredients in nesting dry measuring cups (usually made of metal or plastic) that can be levelled off with a straightedge, such as a knife.

- Measure flour by spooning, not scooping, it into a dry measuring cup. Level off with a straightedge without tapping or shaking cup. Do not sift flour unless directed to in recipe. If flour is substituted, there may be a change in texture.

- Measure brown sugar by packing it firmly enough into a dry measuring cup so that it holds the shape of the cup when turned out.

- In recipes calling for butter, do not use soft tub margarine or vegetable oil as a substitute as this may adversely affect the final product.

- Butter and cream cheese are allowed to soften at room temperature for easier creaming.

- Egg whites will give a greater volume if allowed to stand at room temperature for 30 minutes before beating.

- Whipping cream will whip faster if both bowl and beaters are chilled in the freezer for 15 minutes.

- Use chocolate chips made from pure chocolate. All chocolate chips are formulated to keep their shape in baking and may not melt smoothly for use in cakes and tortes. Imitation chocolate-flavoured chips may be very difficult to melt.

- Unless otherwise specified, do not use light (lite) products (cream cheese, sour cream, mayonnaise, peanut butter, etc.) as they may give poor results due to differences in fat and moisture content.

- All fruits and vegetables must be thoroughly washed before using; carrots, onions, shallots, parsnips, garlic and fresh ginger should be peeled.

- Hot peppers cause severe skin and eye irritation. Wear disposable gloves when handling hot peppers and avoid touching any exposed skin.

- A baking pan refers to a metal pan, while a baking dish refers to a glass or ceramic dish.

- When measuring the dimensions of baking pans and baking dishes, measure the distance across the top from the inside rim on one side to the inside rim on the opposite side.

- Frypans may be classified in size as small, medium or large. Usually, small frypans are 5 – 8 inches in diameter; medium frypans are 9 – 10 inches in diameter; and large frypans are about 12 inches in diameter.

- Unless otherwise specified in the recipe, always cook, roast or bake in a preheated oven or preheated barbecue. Follow the doneness tests described in the recipes. Cooking times should be used only as a guideline.

Table of Contents

Cheesy Tomato Breakfast Scones

Rhubarb Streusel Muffins

Breakfast

Cheesy Tomato Breakfast Scones

Ingredients:

1 cup all-purpose flour

1 cup whole wheat flour

1¼ tsp baking powder

½ tsp baking soda

1 cup salted butter, chilled and cubed

1 cup old-fashioned rolled oats

1 cup crumbled feta cheese

½ cup freshly grated Parmesan cheese

½ cup chopped sun-dried tomatoes

½ cup sliced green onions

1 cup buttermilk

2 tbsp whipping cream

Makes about 12

1. Preheat oven to 350°F.

2. Place flour, whole wheat flour, baking powder and baking soda in a food processor; process to combine. Add butter and process, using an on/off motion, until mixture resembles coarse meal.

3. Transfer mixture to a bowl. Add oats, feta cheese, Parmesan cheese, tomatoes and green onions; stir to combine. Add buttermilk and stir just until combined.

4. Turn dough out onto a lightly floured surface. Knead dough gently and roll out ¾ inch thick. Using a floured 3 inch round cookie cutter, cut dough into rounds.

5. Place rounds on a parchment paper-lined large rimmed baking sheet. Cover and freeze for 10 minutes. This helps the scones keep their shape.

6. Remove baking sheet from freezer and uncover scones. Brush tops with cream. Bake for 25 – 30 minutes or until light golden.

Nutritional analysis per scone:
306 calories, 21.2 g fat, 7.4 g protein, 23.1 g carbohydrate, 2.6 g fibre, 484 mg sodium

Brisket Hash

For a special brunch, top each serving of this dish with a poached or fried egg.

Ingredients:

4 cups cubed unpeeled yellow potatoes (1 inch)

3 tbsp canola oil, divided

2 cups julienned red onions

1½ cups julienned red bell peppers

3 cloves garlic, finely chopped

4 cups shredded *Pressure Cooker Beef Brisket (recipe on page 77)*

1 cup sliced green onions

1 tbsp chopped fresh rosemary or 1 tsp dried rosemary, crumbled

Serves 6

1. Cook potatoes in boiling salted water until tender; drain and set aside.

2. Heat 1 tbsp oil in a large non-stick frypan over medium-high heat. Add red onions and red peppers; sauté, until softened, about 5 minutes.

3. Add garlic and cook, stirring, until fragrant, about 1 minute. Remove from heat and transfer red onion mixture to a plate; set aside.

4. Heat 1 tbsp oil in same frypan over medium-high heat. Add potatoes and sauté until golden brown, about 9 – 10 minutes.

5. Add remaining 1 tbsp oil to frypan with potatoes. Add Pressure Cooker Beef Brisket and stir to combine; cook, without stirring, until brisket is browned on bottom, about 1 – 2 minutes.

6. Return red onion mixture to frypan. Add green onions and rosemary; cook, stirring, until combined and heated through.

Nutritional analysis per serving:
477 calories, 31.3 g fat, 25.6 g protein, 22.8 g carbohydrate, 3.9 g fibre, 319 mg sodium

Rhubarb Streusel Muffins

1. Preheat oven to 350°F.

2. To prepare topping, combine pecans, sugar, butter and cinnamon until mixture is crumbly; set aside. Combine flour, baking soda and salt in a bowl.

3. Whisk together brown sugar, sour cream, oil and egg in a separate bowl until blended. Add sour cream mixture to flour mixture and stir just until combined. Fold in rhubarb.

4. Spoon batter into paper-lined or greased muffin cups, filling cups three-quarters full. Sprinkle each with topping.

5. Bake for 25 minutes or until a cake tester inserted in centres comes out clean.

6. Cool muffins in pan for 10 minutes. Remove from pan and cool on a rack. May be frozen.

Nutritional analysis per muffin:
266 calories, 10.2 g fat, 3.5 g protein, 39.7 g carbohydrate, 1.1 g fibre, 229 mg sodium

Ingredients:

¼ cup chopped pecans

¼ cup granulated sugar

1 tbsp salted butter, softened

¾ tsp cinnamon

2 cups all-purpose flour

1 tsp baking soda

½ tsp salt

1 cup packed golden brown sugar

¾ cup sour cream

¼ cup canola oil

1 large egg

1¼ cups fresh or frozen diced rhubarb

Makes 12

Bacon Cinnamon Pancakes

1. Combine flour, baking soda, baking powder, cinnamon and salt in a bowl; set aside.

2. Sauté bacon in a large non-stick frypan over medium heat until browned and crisp. Remove from heat. Remove bacon with a slotted spoon; drain bacon on paper towels and set aside. Drain off and reserve 1 tbsp fat from frypan; cool slightly.

3. Whisk together reserved 1 tbsp fat, milk, yogurt, eggs, cooled melted butter and vanilla until blended. Add milk mixture to flour mixture and stir just until combined. Do not overmix.

4. Using ⅓ cup batter for each pancake, spoon batter, spreading lightly, onto a lightly greased griddle or non-stick frypan over medium heat. Sprinkle each with about 1 tbsp bacon.

5. Cook pancakes until golden brown, about 2 – 3 minutes per side. Serve with maple syrup.

Nutritional analysis per pancake:
158 calories, 6.9 g fat, 6.4 g protein, 16.8 g carbohydrate, 0.6 g fibre, 479 mg sodium

*Ingredient not included in nutritional analysis.

Ingredients:

2 cups all-purpose flour

2 tsp baking soda

1 tsp baking powder

1 tsp cinnamon

½ tsp salt

1½ cups chopped bacon

1 cup milk (2%)

¾ cup plain yogurt

3 large eggs

2 tbsp salted butter, melted and cooled

2 tsp vanilla

Maple syrup*

Makes about 13

Ingredients:

¼ cup *Roasted Red Pepper Mayo (recipe follows)*

8 slices *Everyday Bread (recipe on page 100)* or white bread, toasted

½ cup arugula

2 ready-to-serve deli chorizo sausages (about 125 g each)

4 large eggs

8 slices Manchego cheese

Makes 4

Did You Know?

Arugula is a salad green with a bitter peppery taste. Look for it in the produce section of grocery stores.

Fried Egg and Chorizo Sandwiches

These sandwiches are also great with our Rye Bread (recipe on page 102).

1. Spread Roasted Red Pepper Mayo on one side of bread slices, dividing equally. Top each of 4 bread slices with arugula, dividing equally; set all bread slices aside.

2. Cut each sausage lengthwise into 4 slices. Cut each slice crosswise into 2 pieces. There should be 16 pieces. Heat a large non-stick frypan over medium heat. Add sausage pieces and cook, turning occasionally, until browned and heated through.

3. Transfer sausage pieces to a paper towel-lined plate; set aside. Drain off all but 1 tsp fat from frypan.

4. Crack eggs into frypan and cook over medium heat to desired doneness. Flip eggs over. Top each egg with 2 slices of cheese. Cover frypan and cook until cheese is melted. Remove from heat.

5. Place 1 fried egg on each arugula-topped bread slice. Top each fried egg with 4 sausage pieces. Cover with remaining bread slices. Serve immediately.

Nutritional analysis per sandwich:
637 calories, 42.6 g fat, 35.6 g protein, 27.9 g carbohydrate, 1.4 g fibre, 1520 mg sodium

 Cook's Note: Manchego cheese is a richly flavoured Spanish cheese. Look for it in the deli department of large grocery stores.

Roasted Red Pepper Mayo

1. Place roasted peppers, green onion, lemon juice, garlic and cayenne pepper in a mini food processor; process, using an on/off motion, until almost smooth.

2. Transfer roasted pepper mixture to a bowl. Add mayonnaise and stir to combine. May be refrigerated for up to 24 hours. Makes about 1 cup.

Nutritional analysis per 1 tbsp serving:
52 calories, 5.5 g fat, 0.2 g protein, 0.7 g carbohydrate, 0.1 g fibre, 58 mg sodium

Ingredients:

½ cup chopped drained roasted red peppers, patted dry

2 tbsp sliced green onion

1 tbsp fresh lemon juice

2 cloves garlic, finely chopped

½ tsp cayenne pepper

½ cup mayonnaise

Fried Egg and Chorizo Sandwiches

Ingredients:

1 tbsp canola oil

1 cup diced onion

1 cup diced red bell pepper

½ cup frozen kernel corn

1 can (14 oz/398 mL) black beans, rinsed and drained

½ cup water

1 tsp chili powder

1 tsp ground cumin

1 tsp oregano, crumbled

1 tsp salt

½ tsp freshly ground pepper

8 large eggs

1 tbsp canola oil

8 whole wheat flour tortillas (10 inch)

½ cup shredded aged white cheddar cheese

2 Roma tomatoes, cored and diced

1 ripe avocado, diced

¼ cup chopped fresh cilantro

Makes 8

Black Bean Breakfast Wraps

1. Heat 1 tbsp oil in a large non-stick frypan over medium heat. Add onion and red pepper; sauté until softened, about 2 minutes.

2. Add corn and cook, stirring, until heated through. Remove from heat.

3. Transfer onion mixture to a plate; set aside.

4. Add beans, water, chili powder, cumin, oregano, salt and pepper to same frypan; stir to combine. Bring to a simmer over medium heat and cook, uncovered, stirring occasionally, until water is evaporated, about 5 minutes. Remove from heat.

5. Partially mash bean mixture with a potato masher; set aside.

6. Whisk together eggs until blended.

7. To scramble eggs, heat 1 tbsp oil in a medium non-stick frypan over medium heat. Add eggs and cook, uncovered, lifting edges of eggs occasionally with a spatula, allowing uncooked eggs to run underneath, until eggs are cooked through. Remove from heat.

8. Spread about ¼ cup bean mixture down centre of each tortilla. Top each with ¼ cup onion mixture, ¼ cup scrambled eggs and 1 tbsp cheese. Dividing equally, sprinkle each with tomatoes, avocado and cilantro. Roll up tortillas to enclose filling.

Nutritional analysis per wrap:
408 calories, 14.7 g fat, 18.5 g protein, 53.6 g carbohydrate, 10 g fibre, 790 mg sodium

 Safety Matters: If you move into an older home with electric appliances in place, check behind them for uncapped natural gas lines or valves. If you find an uncapped gas line or aren't sure what you are looking for, contact a qualified gas fitter, a heating contractor or ATCO Gas. Learn more at atcogas.com.

Ingredients:

2 cups sliced nectarines

2 cups sliced peaches

½ cup sliced apricots

1 tbsp granulated sugar

1 tbsp salted butter

1 tsp vanilla

Basic Pannekoek (recipe follows)

1 cup crumbled soft goat cheese

Maple syrup*

Makes 6

Pannekoek with Summer Fruit and Goat Cheese

A pannekoek is a large, thin Dutch pancake that can be topped with sweet or savoury ingredients. In this version, they are topped with fruit and goat cheese and then rolled.

1. Combine nectarines, peaches, apricots and sugar in a bowl.

2. Melt butter in a large non-stick frypan over medium-high heat. Add fruit mixture and sauté until fruit is slightly softened, about 3 – 4 minutes. Remove from heat and stir in vanilla.

3. Place fruit down centre of each pannekoek, dividing equally. Top each with cheese, dividing equally. Roll up to enclose filling.

4. Serve drizzled with maple syrup.

Nutritional analysis per filled pannekoek:
414 calories, 22.7 g fat, 17.7 g protein, 34.7 g carbohydrate, 2.4 g fibre, 347 mg sodium

*Ingredient not included in nutritional analysis.

Ingredients:

2 cups milk (2%)

1 cup all-purpose flour

4 large eggs

2 tsp vanilla

¼ tsp salt

3 tbsp canola oil

Basic Pannekoek

1. Whisk together milk, flour, eggs, vanilla and salt until smooth.

2. Heat 1 tbsp oil in a 10 inch non-stick frypan over medium-high heat. Pour ½ cup batter in frypan. Swirl frypan until it is coated on bottom with batter; cook until underside is golden brown, about 1 minute.

3. Loosen edges of pannekoek with a spatula. Slide spatula under pannekoek and quickly flip it over; cook until underside is golden brown, about 1 minute.

4. Gently slide pannekoek onto a parchment paper-lined large rimmed baking sheet.

5. Repeat procedure with remaining batter, adding remaining oil as necessary.

6. Pannekoek may be cooled and frozen for up to 1 month. If freezing, layer pannekoek with parchment paper in an airtight container. Makes 6.

Nutritional analysis per pannekoek:
230 calories, 12 g fat, 9 g protein, 20.2 g carbohydrate, 0.6 g fibre, 183 mg sodium

Cheddar Prosciutto Stuffed Fren[...]

Ingredients:

8 slices French bread (½ inch)

8 slices aged white cheddar cheese

4 slices prosciutto

¼ cup crumbled soft goat cheese

4 large eggs

2 tbsp light cream (10%)

⅛ tsp salt

Pinch cayenne pepper

2 tbsp salted butter

*Tomato Rhubarb Compote (recipe follows)**

Serves 4

1. Top each of 4 bread slices with 2 slices white cheddar cheese, 1 slice prosciutto and 1 tbsp goat cheese. Cover with remaining bread slices; set aside.

2. Whisk together eggs, cream, salt and cayenne pepper in a shallow bowl until blended.

3. Melt butter in a large non-stick frypan over medium heat.

4. Working with one sandwich at a time, dip sandwiches into egg mixture, turning to coat both sides.

5. Cook sandwiches in frypan until they are golden brown and cheese is melted, about 3 minutes per side.

6. Serve with Tomato Rhubarb Compote.

Nutritional analysis per serving:
573 calories, 35.5 g fat, 33.2 g protein, 30 g carbohydrate, 1.2 g fibre, 1175 mg sodium

*Ingredient not included in nutritional analysis.

Tomato Rhubarb Compote

Ingredients:

1 tbsp salted butter

1 cup diced onion

3 cups fresh or frozen diced rhubarb

2 cups diced seeded Roma tomatoes

½ cup dry white wine

½ cup liquid honey

¼ cup sherry vinegar

1 tsp chopped fresh rosemary

⅛ tsp salt

1. Melt butter in a medium non-reactive saucepan over medium heat. Add onion and sauté until softened, about 5 minutes.

2. Add rhubarb, tomatoes, wine, honey, vinegar, rosemary and salt; stir to combine. Bring to a boil.

3. Reduce heat and simmer, uncovered, stirring occasionally, until rhubarb is broken down and mixture is thickened, about 40 – 45 minutes.

4. Serve warm or cold. May be refrigerated for up to 3 days or frozen for up to 1 month. Makes about 2 cups.

Nutritional analysis per 1 tbsp serving:
30 calories, 0.4 g fat, 0.3 g protein, 6.4 g carbohydrate, 0.4 g fibre, 15 mg sodium

 To learn how to make Tomato Rhubarb Compote, visit our YouTube channel at youtube.com/TheBlueFlameKitchen

Coddled Eggs with Prosciutto

Coddling is a cooking method where food is typically put in heatproof dishes that are covered and gently cooked in a water bath either in the oven or on the stove.

1. Preheat oven to 400°F.

2. Place prosciutto in a parchment paper-lined rimmed baking sheet.

3. Bake until prosciutto is crisp, about 15 minutes.

4. Transfer prosciutto to a paper towel-lined plate; cool. Break 2 prosciutto slices in half; set aside for garnishing.

5. Transfer remaining 3 prosciutto slices to a cutting board. Chop prosciutto; set aside.

6. Preheat oven to 375°F.

7. Place 1 tbsp cheese, ½ tbsp Kale Pesto and ½ tbsp tomatoes in each of four ¾ cup heatproof ramekins. Sprinkle each with chopped prosciutto, dividing equally. Crack 2 eggs on top of mixture in each ramekin.

8. Place ramekins in a 9 inch square baking pan. Pour enough hot water into pan to come halfway up sides of ramekins.

9. Bake, covered, until eggs are set, about 30 minutes.

10. Uncover and remove ramekins from pan. Top each with remaining cheese, Kale Pesto and tomatoes, dividing equally. Garnish each with 1 prosciutto half.

Nutritional analysis per serving:
319 calories, 23.5 g fat, 22.7 g protein, 3.9 g carbohydrate, 0.8 g fibre, 602 mg sodium

Ingredients:

5 slices prosciutto

½ cup crumbled soft goat cheese, divided

¼ cup *Kale Pesto (recipe on page 86)* or basil pesto, divided

¼ cup chopped drained oil-packed sun-dried tomatoes, patted dry, divided

8 large eggs

Serves 4

 Did you know? A natural gas water heater will save you about $4,000, versus electric, over the life of the appliance. Learn more at atcogas.com.

Italian Sausage and Potato Frittata

Ingredients:

3 tbsp extra-virgin olive oil, divided

2 mild Italian sausages (about 100 g each), sliced (¼ inch)

3 cups sliced onions

2½ cups sliced peeled yellow potatoes (¼ inch)

8 large eggs

1 tbsp chopped fresh parsley

1 tsp paprika

½ tsp salt

½ tsp freshly ground pepper

1 cup freshly grated Parmesan cheese

¾ cup diced red bell pepper

1 tbsp chopped fresh parsley

Serves 8

 To learn how to make sausage and potato frittata, visit our YouTube channel at youtube.com/TheBlueFlameKitchen

1. Preheat oven to 425°F.

2. Heat 1 tbsp oil in a 10 inch cast iron frypan over medium heat. Add sausages and cook, stirring, until browned and cooked through.

3. Transfer sausages to a paper towel-lined plate; set aside. Drain off excess fat from frypan.

4. Heat remaining 2 tbsp oil in same frypan over medium-high heat. Add onions and potatoes; carefully sauté for 3 minutes.

5. Reduce heat and cook, covered, stirring occasionally, until onions and potatoes are softened and golden brown, about 20 minutes.

6. Meanwhile, whisk together eggs, 1 tbsp parsley, paprika, salt and pepper in a bowl until blended. Stir in Parmesan cheese; set aside.

7. Return sausages to frypan; stir to combine.

8. Pour egg mixture over sausage mixture. Sprinkle with red pepper. Remove from heat.

9. Bake until frittata is set and lightly browned, about 20 minutes.

10. Let stand for 20 minutes before serving.

11. Sprinkle with 1 tbsp parsley. Cut into wedges and serve.

Nutritional analysis per serving:
278 calories, 17.8 g fat, 14.2 g protein, 14.6 g carbohydrate, 1.9 g fibre, 523 mg sodium

 Safety Matters: If natural gas flames continuously burn yellow at the tips, turn the burner off, allow the grid to cool and ensure the burner holes are free of debris. If the problem persists contact a qualified technician to have the unit serviced. For more safety tips, visit atcogas.com.

Italian Sausage and Potato Frittata

Apple Cinnamon Steel-Cut Oats

Ingredients:

2 tbsp salted butter

1 cup steel-cut oats

4 cups water

1 cinnamon stick or ⅛ tsp cinnamon

½ vanilla bean or ⅛ tsp vanilla

¼ tsp salt

1 apple, cored and diced

1 cup raisins

Milk (2%)*

Maple syrup*

Serves 4

1. Melt butter in a medium saucepan over medium heat. Add oats and cook, stirring constantly, until fragrant, about 4 minutes.

2. Add water, cinnamon stick, vanilla bean and salt; stir to combine. Bring to a boil.

3. Reduce heat and simmer, uncovered, stirring occasionally, for 30 minutes.

4. Stir in apple and raisins; cook, uncovered, stirring occasionally, until liquid is absorbed, about 8 – 10 minutes. Remove from heat; remove and discard cinnamon stick and vanilla bean.

5. Serve topped with milk and maple syrup.

Nutritional analysis per serving:
319 calories, 8.4 g fat, 7.1 g protein, 61.3 g carbohydrate, 6.3 g fibre, 200 mg sodium

*Ingredient not included in nutritional analysis.

Cook's Note: Steel-cut oats are oat groats that are cut up but not rolled, whereas rolled oats are oat groats that are steamed and rolled flat. The cooking time is longer for steel-cut oats, which have a chewy texture when ready to eat. Look for them in natural food stores, specialty food stores or large grocery stores in the natural foods section or the aisle where oats are sold.

Chilled Strawberry Rhubarb Soup

Soups & More

Ingredients:

1 can (400 mL) coconut milk

1½ cups chopped strawberries

1 cup fresh or frozen sliced rhubarb

½ cup water

¼ cup liquid honey

2 tbsp fresh lime juice

1 tbsp finely chopped fresh ginger

2 kaffir lime leaves or 1 tsp grated lime peel

1 piece lemon grass stalk (2 inch), bruised

½ jalapeno pepper, seeded

⅛ tsp salt

Pinch cayenne pepper

Serves 4 as a starter

Did You Know?

Even though rhubarb stalks are edible, their leaves aren't as they contain oxalic acid, which is toxic. After a frost, the toxin can move to the rhubarb stalk, making it inedible. Before harvesting rhubarb, check if the leaves are damaged, which may be an indicator of a frost.

Chilled Strawberry Rhubarb Soup

This sweet summer soup makes a lovely appetizer for a small group.

1. Combine all ingredients in a medium non-reactive saucepan. Bring to a boil over medium heat.

2. Reduce heat and simmer, uncovered, stirring occasionally, for 15 minutes. Remove from heat; remove and discard lime leaves, lemon grass and jalapeno.

3. Purée mixture in batches in a blender, filling blender no more than half full for each batch.

4. Transfer to a heatproof bowl and cool to room temperature, stirring occasionally. Cover and refrigerate until cold or for up to 24 hours.

5. Stir before serving.

Nutritional analysis per serving:
272 calories, 19.6 g fat, 2.6 g protein, 27 g carbohydrate, 2.8 g fibre, 91 mg sodium

 Building or renovating a home? Save money with natural gas appliances! Learn more at atcogas.com.

...n Squash and Apple Soup

1. Preheat oven to 375°F.

2. Place squash halves, cut side down, in a parchment paper-lined rimmed baking sheet.

3. Bake until squash is tender, about 40 – 45 minutes.

4. When cool enough to handle, scoop squash from shell halves; discard shell halves. There should be about 4 cups squash; set aside.

5. Melt 2 tbsp butter in a Dutch oven over medium-high heat. Add apples and sauté until tender and lightly browned, about 8 minutes.

6. Transfer apples to a plate; set aside.

7. Melt remaining 1 tbsp butter in same Dutch oven over medium heat. Add onions, celery and garlic; sauté until softened, about 5 minutes.

8. Add squash, broth, ginger, cinnamon and nutmeg; stir to combine. Bring to a boil.

9. Reduce heat and simmer, uncovered, stirring occasionally, for 30 minutes.

10. Return apples to Dutch oven; stir to combine. Stir in apple juice, honey and salt; cook, stirring, until heated through. Stir in cream. Remove from heat.

11. Using a hand blender, purée mixture until smooth.

12. Serve topped with yogurt and green onion.

Nutritional analysis per serving:
321 calories, 10.9 g fat, 4.4 g protein, 55.8 g carbohydrate, 10.8 g fibre, 1095 mg sodium

*Ingredient not included in nutritional analysis.

Ingredients:

1 large acorn squash (about 2 lb), halved lengthwise and seeded

3 tbsp salted butter, divided

4 cups diced peeled apples

2 cups chopped onions

1½ cups chopped celery

5 cloves garlic, finely chopped

6 cups no-salt-added vegetable broth

2 tsp ground ginger

1 tsp cinnamon

1 tsp nutmeg

1 cup apple juice

2 tbsp liquid honey

2½ tsp salt

1 cup light cream (10%)

Plain yogurt*

Sliced green onion*

Serves 6

 Safety Matters: If there is an oven fire, turn off the heat and keep the door closed until the flames are extinguished. For more safety tips, visit atcogas.com.

Mushroom Soup Cappuccinos

This appetizer soup mimics a cappuccino as it's served in small cappuccino cups and topped with whipped cream.

Ingredients:

1 pkg (14 g) dried mushrooms, rinsed and drained (about ½ cup)

1 cup boiling water

2 tbsp canola oil

2 cups sliced mushrooms

½ cup chopped celery

½ cup chopped onion

2 sprigs fresh thyme

2 bay leaves

½ cup dry white wine

4 cups no-salt-added chicken broth

½ cup whipping cream

2 tsp sherry vinegar

½ tsp salt

Whipped cream or sour cream*

Serves 6 as a starter

Did You Know?

When puréeing hot mixtures in a blender, the buildup of steam and pressure inside the blender may cause the lid to blow off. To avoid this, purée in small batches; the blender should be no more than half full. Let the mixture cool, uncovered, in the blender for a few minutes before blending. Remove the centre piece of the lid and then place the lid on the blender. Holding a folded clean tea towel firmly over the lid, start blending at low speed. Increase speed to high and continue blending until mixture is smooth.

1. Place dried mushrooms in a heatproof bowl. Pour boiling water over dried mushrooms. Let stand for 20 minutes.

2. Meanwhile, heat oil in a Dutch oven over medium-high heat. Add sliced mushrooms and sauté for 3 minutes.

3. Reduce heat to medium and add celery, onion, thyme and bay leaves; sauté until vegetables are softened, about 4 minutes.

4. Add wine and cook, stirring, until wine is almost evaporated. Add broth, soaked dried mushrooms and liquid; stir to combine. Bring to a boil.

5. Reduce heat and simmer, uncovered, stirring occasionally, for 20 minutes.

6. Stir in cream. Remove from heat; remove and discard thyme and bay leaves.

7. Purée mixture in batches in a blender, filling blender no more than half full for each batch.

8. Stir in vinegar and salt.

9. Serve in small cappuccino or tea cups with a dollop of whipped cream.

Nutritional analysis per serving:
170 calories, 13.2 g fat, 4.9 g protein, 5.6 g carbohydrate, 0.9 g fibre, 298 mg sodium

*Ingredient not included in nutritional analysis.

 Enjoy warm summer nights on the patio year-round with a natural gas patio heater. Visit atcogas.com.

Mushroom Soup Cappuccinos

Ingredients:

1 cup dried white kidney beans, rinsed and drained

3 cups cold water

½ cup diced pancetta

1 cup chopped onion

½ cup chopped carrot

½ cup chopped celery

1½ tsp basil, crumbled

1 tsp oregano, crumbled

½ tsp marjoram, crumbled

3 cloves garlic, finely chopped

1 bay leaf

¼ cup dry white wine

4 cups no-salt-added chicken broth or vegetable broth

1 can (28 oz/796 mL) diced tomatoes

1 cup small shell pasta or macaroni

½ cup slivered fresh basil

½ tsp freshly ground pepper

¼ tsp salt

Extra-virgin olive oil*

½ cup freshly grated Parmesan cheese

Serves 5

 To learn how to make pasta e fagioli using a pressure cooker, visit our YouTube channel at youtube.com/TheBlueFlameKitchen

Pressure Cooker Pasta e Fagioli

Pasta e fagioli is a hearty Italian soup. The name literally means "pasta and beans".

1. Place beans in a large non-reactive bowl. Pour cold water over beans. Cover and refrigerate overnight.

2. Drain beans and set aside.

3. Sauté pancetta in a 6 quart pressure cooker over medium heat until browned and crisp. Add onion, carrot, celery, basil, oregano, marjoram, garlic and bay leaf; sauté until vegetables are softened, about 5 minutes.

4. Add wine and cook, stirring, until wine is almost evaporated. Add soaked beans and broth; stir to combine. Cover with lid and lock it in place. Bring to high pressure over high heat.

5. Cook for 17 minutes, adjusting heat as needed to maintain high pressure.

6. Carefully remove from heat and allow steam to release naturally. This may take 10 – 15 minutes.

7. Wearing oven mitts, carefully open lid away from yourself to protect from steam. Add tomatoes and stir to combine. Bring to a boil over medium heat.

8. Reduce heat and stir in pasta. Simmer, uncovered, stirring occasionally, until beans and pasta are tender. Stir in fresh basil, pepper and salt. Remove from heat; remove and discard bay leaf.

9. Serve drizzled with oil and topped with Parmesan cheese. As the pasta absorbs liquid, this soup is best served immediately.

Nutritional analysis per serving:
413 calories, 12.3 g fat, 25.4 g protein, 50.7 g carbohydrate, 12.9 g fibre, 1048 mg sodium

*Ingredient not included in nutritional analysis.

 Cook's Note: White kidney beans are also known as cannellini beans. Look for dried white kidney beans in specialty food stores.

Dried red and white kidney beans contain naturally occurring plant proteins called lectins. It is important to fully cook all dried kidney beans as lectins are toxic and can cause sickness.

White Bean and Rosemary Soup

1. Place thyme sprigs, rosemary sprigs, peppercorns and bay leaf on a piece of cheesecloth. Gather cheesecloth around herbs and peppercorns, folding herbs over if needed, to form a sachet. Tie with butcher's twine. The sachet allows the herbs and peppercorns to be easily removed from the soup before serving.

2. Melt butter in a Dutch oven over medium heat. Add herb sachet, celery, onion and garlic; sauté until vegetables are softened and lightly browned, about 10 minutes.

3. Add wine and cook, stirring, until wine is almost evaporated. Add beans and broth; stir to combine. Bring to a boil.

4. Reduce heat and simmer, uncovered, stirring occasionally, for 30 minutes. Remove from heat; remove and discard herb sachet.

5. Purée mixture in batches in a blender, filling blender no more than half full for each batch.

6. Add yogurt, chopped rosemary, pepper and salt; stir to combine.

Nutritional analysis per serving:
295 calories, 8.3 g fat, 19.7 g protein, 34.9 g carbohydrate, 9.1 g fibre, 642 mg sodium

Ingredients:

4 sprigs fresh thyme (3 inch)

2 sprigs fresh rosemary (3 inch)

3 black peppercorns

1 bay leaf

1 tbsp salted butter

1½ cups diced celery

1 cup diced onion

3 cloves garlic, finely chopped

¼ cup dry white wine

2 cans (19 oz/540 mL each) white kidney beans, rinsed and drained

8 cups no-salt-added chicken broth or vegetable broth

1 cup plain Greek yogurt

1 tsp chopped fresh rosemary

¾ tsp freshly ground pepper

½ tsp salt

Serves 6

 Safety Matters: If a natural gas burner fails to light when you turn the control knob to the ignition position, allow the gas to disperse before attempting to light the burner again. For more safety tips, visit atcogas.com.

Ingredients:

2½ tbsp canola oil, divided

1½ lb (0.75 kg) boneless lamb, cut into
  1 inch cubes

1 cup chopped celery

1 cup chopped onion

1 cup cubed carrots (1 inch)

1 cup cubed parsnip (1 inch)

1 cup cubed turnip (1 inch)

1 clove garlic, finely chopped

2 bay leaves

½ cup salted butter

½ cup all-purpose flour

4 cups no-salt-added chicken broth

1½ cups stout or other strong dark beer

1 cup cubed peeled potato (1 inch)

2 tbsp chopped fresh parsley

1 tbsp chopped fresh rosemary

2 tsp fresh lemon juice

1 tsp salt

½ tsp freshly ground pepper

Serves 4

Irish Lamb Stew

1. Heat 1½ tbsp oil in a Dutch oven over medium-high heat. Add lamb in batches and brown on all sides.

2. Transfer lamb to a plate; set aside.

3. Heat remaining 1 tbsp oil in same Dutch oven over medium heat. Add celery, onion, carrots, parsnip and turnip; sauté until softened, about 8 – 9 minutes.

4. Add garlic and bay leaves; sauté for 2 minutes.

5. Add butter and cook, stirring, until butter is melted. Add flour and cook, stirring, for 2 minutes.

6. Add broth, 1 cup at a time, cooking and stirring constantly. Gradually stir in stout.

7. Return lamb and any accumulated juices to Dutch oven; stir to combine. Bring to a boil.

8. Reduce heat and simmer, covered, stirring occasionally, until lamb is tender, about 45 – 60 minutes.

9. Add potato and stir to combine; simmer, uncovered, stirring occasionally, until potato is tender, about 25 – 30 minutes. Remove from heat; remove and discard bay leaves.

10. Stir in parsley, rosemary, lemon juice, salt and pepper.

Nutritional analysis per serving:
729 calories, 42.7 g fat, 43.9 g protein, 36.8 g carbohydrate, 5.4 g fibre, 1103 mg sodium

 Cook's Note: ATCO Blue Flame Kitchen used most of a 440 mL can of Guinness Draught for the stout.

Irish Lamb Stew

Ingredients:

1 tbsp grapeseed oil or canola oil

1 ready-to-serve deli chorizo sausage (about 125 g), diced

2 cups diced onions

1 cup diced carrots

1 cup diced celery

1 cup diced red bell pepper

1 can (5½ oz/156 mL) tomato paste

2 tbsp smoked paprika

3 cloves garlic, finely chopped

1 cup dry white wine

6 cups no-salt-added chicken broth

1¼ cups dried green lentils, rinsed and drained

4 sprigs fresh thyme

2 bay leaves

2 tbsp fresh lemon juice

1 tbsp liquid honey

½ tsp salt

½ tsp freshly ground pepper

Serves 5

Did You Know?

Chorizo is a seasoned, spicy pork sausage used in Spanish and Mexican cooking. Chorizo sausage sold in the deli department of grocery stores is fully cooked and ready to serve. It is different than raw chorizo sausage, which is sold in the meat refrigerator case of grocery stores.

Lentil Chorizo Soup

1. Heat oil in a Dutch oven over medium heat. Add chorizo and sauté until lightly browned, about 2 minutes.

2. Add onions, carrots, celery and red pepper; sauté until vegetables are softened, about 5 – 6 minutes.

3. Add tomato paste, paprika and garlic; sauté for 2 minutes.

4. Add wine and cook, stirring, until wine is reduced by half, about 2 minutes.

5. Add broth, lentils, thyme and bay leaves; stir to combine. Bring to a boil.

6. Reduce heat and simmer, uncovered, stirring occasionally, until lentils are tender, about 40 – 45 minutes. Remove from heat; remove and discard thyme and bay leaves.

7. Stir in lemon juice, honey, salt and pepper.

Nutritional analysis per serving:
436 calories, 12.6 g fat, 25.6 g protein, 50.7 g carbohydrate, 15.5 g fibre, 1006 mg sodium

 Dry clothes faster and save money with a natural gas dryer. Find more benefits of using natural gas at atcogas.com.

Roasted Cauliflower Soup

1. Preheat oven to 400°F.

2. Combine cauliflower, oil and ½ tsp salt in a bowl; toss until coated.

3. Place cauliflower in a single layer in a parchment paper-lined rimmed baking sheet.

4. Bake until cauliflower is tender and lightly browned, about 20 – 25 minutes.

5. Cool cauliflower in pan on a rack.

6. Melt butter in a Dutch oven over medium heat. Add onion and celery; sauté until softened, about 5 minutes.

7. Add potatoes, broth and thyme; stir to combine. Bring to a boil.

8. Reduce heat and simmer, uncovered, stirring occasionally, until potatoes are tender, about 15 minutes.

9. Add cauliflower and stir to combine; cook, stirring, until cauliflower is heated through. Stir in cream. Remove from heat; remove and discard thyme.

10. Using a hand blender, purée mixture until smooth.

11. Stir in lemon juice and ½ tsp salt.

Nutritional analysis per serving:
354 calories, 26.2 g fat, 11.3 g protein, 22 g carbohydrate, 4.9 g fibre, 853 mg sodium

Ingredients:

8 cups cauliflower florets

2 tbsp olive oil

½ tsp salt

2 tbsp salted butter

1 cup chopped onion

½ cup chopped celery

1 cup cubed peeled yellow potatoes

4 cups no-salt-added chicken broth

3 sprigs fresh thyme

1 cup light cream (10%)

2 tbsp fresh lemon juice

½ tsp salt

Serves 4

Safety Matters: ATCO Gas provides information and safety checks to assist customers in using natural gas safely and wisely. Visit atcogas.com for more information.

Potato and Smoked Gouda Soup

Ingredients:

1 tbsp salted butter

1 tsp canola oil

1½ cups chopped onions

1 cup chopped celery

¾ cup chopped carrot

5 cloves garlic, finely chopped

5 cups cubed peeled yellow potatoes
    (1 inch)

6 cups no-salt-added chicken broth

1 cup shredded smoked Gouda cheese

½ cup milk (2%)

1 tsp salt

½ tsp freshly ground pepper

½ tsp turmeric

Toppings: Shredded smoked Gouda cheese,
    sliced green onion and smoked paprika*

Serves 5

1. Melt butter with oil in a Dutch oven over medium heat. Add onions, celery, carrot and garlic; sauté until softened, about 5 minutes.

2. Add potatoes and broth; stir to combine. Bring to a boil.

3. Reduce heat and simmer, uncovered, stirring occasionally, for 30 minutes.

4. Stir in 1 cup cheese, milk, salt, pepper and turmeric; cook, stirring, for 4 minutes. Remove from heat.

5. Using a hand blender, purée mixture until smooth.

6. Serve topped with toppings.

Nutritional analysis per serving:
335 calories, 13 g fat, 17.3 g protein, 40.2 g carbohydrate, 4.3 g fibre, 774 mg sodium

*Ingredient not included in nutritional analysis.

 Instant, precise heat control – one reason why most chefs prefer to cook with natural gas. Learn more at atcogas.com.

Potato and Smoked Gouda Soup

Ingredients:

⅓ cup plain yogurt

⅓ cup chopped fresh cilantro

1 tbsp canola oil

½ cup sliced celery

½ cup sliced shallots

1 tbsp finely chopped fresh ginger

2 kaffir lime leaves or 1 tsp grated lime peel

1 piece lemon grass stalk (4 inch), bruised

1 tsp coriander seed

1 tbsp Thai yellow curry paste

½ cup dry white wine

2½ cups chopped carrots

4 cups no-salt-added chicken broth

1 can (400 mL) coconut milk

2 tbsp fresh lime juice

1 tbsp liquid honey

½ tsp salt

Serves 6 as a starter

Did You Know?
Kaffir lime leaves are dark green and uniquely shaped. A single leaf looks like two leaves attached together. They can be found fresh, frozen or dried. Look for them in Asian grocery stores.

Carrot Coconut Soup

1. To prepare cilantro yogurt, combine yogurt and cilantro until blended. Cover and refrigerate until serving.

2. Heat oil in a large saucepan over medium heat. Add celery, shallots, ginger, lime leaves, lemon grass and coriander seed; sauté until celery and shallots are softened, about 3 – 4 minutes.

3. Add curry paste and cook, stirring, until fragrant, about 4 – 5 minutes.

4. Add wine and cook, stirring, until wine is almost evaporated. Add carrots and broth; stir to combine. Bring to a boil.

5. Reduce heat and simmer, uncovered, stirring occasionally, until carrots are tender, about 10 minutes.

6. Stir in coconut milk. Bring to a simmer and cook, uncovered, stirring occasionally, for 10 minutes. Remove from heat; remove and discard lime leaves and lemon grass.

7. Purée mixture in batches in a blender, filling blender no more than half full for each batch.

8. Stir in lime juice, honey and salt.

9. Serve topped with cilantro yogurt.

Nutritional analysis per serving:
238 calories, 16.9 g fat, 6.2 g protein, 14.8 g carbohydrate, 2.9 g fibre, 439 mg sodium

 Safety Matters: On a natural gas burner, fit the flame to the pot. Set the flame just high enough to cover the bottom of the pot. Flames that are too high are a fire hazard and waste energy. For more information, visit atcogas.com.

Cajun Cobb Salad

Salads

Ingredients:

2 tbsp Cajun seasoning

1¼ lb (0.625 kg) strip loin steak

2 romaine hearts, halved lengthwise

Pink Peppercorn Buttermilk Dressing (recipe follows), divided

4 hard-cooked large eggs, peeled and sliced

1 ripe avocado, sliced

1 cup thinly sliced radishes

¼ cup thawed frozen kernel corn

¼ cup toasted walnuts, coarsely chopped

¼ cup crumbled blue cheese

Serves 4

Did You Know?

Cobb salad had its beginnings at Hollywood's Brown Derby Restaurant in the 1920s when the restaurant manager, Bob Cobb, came up with it as a delicious way to use up leftovers. Typical ingredients are lettuce, chicken or turkey, vegetables, hard-cooked eggs, bacon and cheese.

Ingredients:

¼ cup buttermilk

2 tbsp fresh lemon juice

2 tsp pink peppercorns, crushed

1½ tsp finely chopped shallot

1½ tsp Dijon mustard

1½ tsp liquid honey

¼ tsp salt

½ cup canola oil

Cajun Cobb Salad

This spicy main dish salad with barbecued steak makes for a great dinner on the patio.

1. Spread Cajun seasoning over both sides of steak.

2. Grill steak over medium heat on natural gas barbecue to desired doneness. Let stand for 5 minutes before slicing.

3. Slice steak into thin slices; set aside.

4. To serve, place 1 romaine heart half on each of 4 individual serving plates. Drizzle each romaine heart half with 2 tbsp Pink Peppercorn Buttermilk Dressing. Dividing equally, add steak, eggs, avocado, radishes, corn, walnuts and blue cheese to plates. Drizzle servings with remaining Pink Peppercorn Buttermilk Dressing. Serve immediately.

Nutritional analysis per serving:
673 calories, 51.1 g fat, 36.3 g protein, 21 g carbohydrate, 8 g fibre, 862 mg sodium

Pink Peppercorn Buttermilk Dressing

1. Place all ingredients except oil in a blender; blend to combine.

2. With machine running, pour oil through opening in lid in a thin steady stream, blending until combined. **Makes about 3/4 cup.**

Nutritional analysis per 1 tbsp serving:
89 calories, 9.3 g fat, 0.3 g protein, 1.5 g carbohydrate, 0.1 g fibre, 70 mg sodium

 Experience warmth and comfort for less with a natural gas high-efficiency furnace. Learn more at atcogas.com.

Warm Lentil Salad

1. Cook potatoes in boiling salted water until tender, adding asparagus for last 2 minutes of cooking; drain and set aside.

2. Combine 4 cups water, lentils, garlic, bay leaf and salt in a large saucepan. Bring to a boil.

3. Reduce heat and simmer, covered, until lentils are tender, about 20 – 25 minutes. Drain; remove and discard garlic and bay leaf.

4. Spread lentils out in a rimmed baking sheet to cool slightly; set aside.

5. To prepare dressing, whisk together vinegar, chives, shallot and mustard until combined. Gradually whisk in ¼ cup oil until blended; set aside.

6. Heat remaining 1 tbsp oil in a large non-stick frypan over medium heat. Add potatoes and asparagus; sauté until warmed, about 2 minutes.

7. Add kale and cook, stirring, until kale wilts slightly, about 30 seconds. Remove from heat.

8. Combine lentils and potato mixture in a bowl.

9. Add dressing and toss to combine. Sprinkle with cheese. Serve immediately.

Nutritional analysis per serving:
234 calories, 11.1 g fat, 9.9 g protein, 26.2 g carbohydrate, 7.4 g fibre, 348 mg sodium

 Cook's Note: Baby kale is more tender and mild in flavour than mature kale. It is often used as a salad green. Look for it in the produce section of grocery stores where packaged greens are sold.

Ingredients:

2½ cups unpeeled baby yellow potatoes, halved

2½ cups sliced asparagus (1 inch)

4 cups water

1 cup dried green lentils, rinsed and drained

1 clove garlic, bruised

1 bay leaf

1 tsp salt

2 tbsp sherry vinegar

2 tbsp finely chopped chives

1 tsp finely chopped shallot

1 tsp Dijon mustard

⅓ cup canola oil, divided

1 pkg (5 oz/142 g) baby kale, chopped

¼ cup crumbled soft goat cheese

Serves 8

Did You Know?

Lentils are small, round and flat and belong to the pulse family. They come in different colours and varieties. They are often used in soups but can also be used in salads and more. Both dried and canned lentils are available in most grocery stores.

Ingredients:

3 cups thinly sliced cabbage (napa, savoy or green)

1 cup julienned carrots

1 cup julienned seeded English cucumber

1 cup julienned seeded Roma tomatoes

Thai Dressing (recipe follows)

3 tbsp chopped fresh cilantro

3 tbsp thinly sliced fresh basil

3 tbsp thinly sliced fresh mint

½ cup unsalted blanched roasted peanuts, toasted and chopped

Serves 4

Ingredients:

¼ cup fresh lime juice

2 tbsp fish sauce

2 tbsp granulated sugar

2 tsp rice vinegar

6 slices fresh ginger, ⅛ inch thick

2 kaffir lime leaves or ½ tsp grated lime peel

1 piece lemon grass stalk (2 inch), chopped

1 clove garlic, bruised

1 sprig cilantro

1 Thai red or green chile pepper, halved and seeded

1 tbsp canola oil

Thai Salad

1. Combine cabbage, carrots, cucumber and tomatoes in a bowl.

2. Add dressing and toss to combine. Let stand for 2 – 3 minutes, tossing occasionally.

3. Add cilantro, basil and mint; toss gently to combine.

4. Serve topped with peanuts. Serve immediately.

Nutritional analysis per serving:
220 calories, 13.8 g fat, 7.4 g protein, 21.1 g carbohydrate, 5.2 g fibre, 674 mg sodium

Thai Dressing

1. Combine all ingredients except oil in a small non-reactive saucepan. Bring to a boil over medium heat. Remove from heat.

2. Transfer mixture to a heatproof bowl and cool to room temperature, stirring occasionally. Cover and refrigerate for at least 1 hour or up to 24 hours.

3. Strain mixture through a sieve into a bowl; discard solids. Gradually whisk in oil until blended. Makes about 1/2 cup.

Nutritional analysis per 1 tbsp serving:
31 calories, 1.8 g fat, 0.2 g protein, 3.8 g carbohydrate, 0 g fibre, 318 mg sodium

 Safety Matters: Since the flames of a natural gas burner can be set at any intensity, and with greater accuracy, it's easier to control heat and prevent food from burning. Learn more at atcogas.com.

Arugula Caprese Salad

Caprese salad is an Italian salad that typically consists of tomatoes, mozzarella and basil.

Ingredients:

2 tbsp white wine vinegar

2 cloves garlic, finely chopped

1 tsp liquid honey

½ tsp salt

½ tsp freshly ground pepper

⅓ cup extra-virgin olive oil

4 cups arugula

2 cups halved grape tomatoes

1¼ cups mini bocconcini

1 cup fresh basil leaves, torn into pieces

Serves 8

1. To prepare dressing, whisk together vinegar, garlic, honey, salt and pepper until combined. Gradually whisk in oil until blended.

2. Combine arugula, tomatoes, bocconcini and basil in a bowl.

3. Add dressing and toss to combine.

Nutritional analysis per serving:
165 calories, 14.2 g fat, 6.8 g protein, 3.4 g carbohydrate, 0.9 g fibre, 301 mg sodium

 Cook's Note: Bocconcini are balls of fresh mozzarella cheese that come packed in water. Look for them in the deli department of large grocery stores.

Egg-Free Caesar Dressing

Toss torn romaine lettuce and croutons with this dressing for a great Caesar salad.

Ingredients:

⅓ cup freshly grated Parmesan cheese

2 tbsp fresh lemon juice

1 tbsp Dijon mustard

1 tbsp drained capers, rinsed

2 cloves garlic, chopped

1½ tsp liquid honey

½ tsp anchovy paste, optional

½ cup extra-virgin olive oil

Makes about 1 cup

1. Place all ingredients except oil in a blender; blend to combine.

2. With machine running, pour oil through opening in lid in a thin steady stream, blending until combined. Cover and refrigerate for at least 1 hour or up to 2 days. Stir before using.

Nutritional analysis per 1 tbsp serving:
70 calories, 7.2 g fat, 0.7 g protein, 1 g carbohydrate, 0.1 g fibre, 71 mg sodium

 Cook's Note: Classic Caesar dressings often call for egg yolks. For food safety reasons, it is not recommended to use eggs in recipes where they remain uncooked or lightly cooked. This recipe is unique as it does not contain egg yolks or mayonnaise, which is often used in egg-free Caesar dressings.

Arugula Caprese Salad

Ingredients:

2 cups fresh or frozen kernel corn

2 tsp chili powder

1 tsp canola oil

1 tbsp fresh lime juice

1 tbsp white wine vinegar

1½ tsp chili powder

1½ tsp liquid honey

¼ tsp salt

⅓ cup canola oil

16 cups torn mixed greens

2 cups shredded cooked chicken

1 can (14 oz/398 mL) black beans, rinsed and drained

1 cup crumbled queso fresco or crumbled feta cheese

1 cup julienned yellow bell pepper

2 Roma tomatoes, cored, seeded and julienned

Serves 6

Fiesta Salad with Roasted Corn

Serve this main dish salad on its own or topped with sour cream, salsa and broken tortilla chips.

1. Preheat oven to 425°F.

2. Combine corn, 2 tsp chili powder and 1 tsp oil in a bowl; toss to coat.

3. Place corn in a single layer in a greased large rimmed baking sheet.

4. Bake until corn is tender and lightly browned, about 15 – 17 minutes.

5. Cool in pan on a rack.

6. To prepare dressing, whisk together lime juice, vinegar, 1½ tsp chili powder, honey and salt until combined. Gradually whisk in ⅓ cup oil until blended.

7. Combine corn, greens, chicken, beans, queso fresco, yellow pepper and tomatoes in a large bowl.

8. Add dressing and toss to coat. Serve immediately.

Nutritional analysis per serving:
390 calories, 21.1 g fat, 25.5 g protein, 28.2 g carbohydrate, 8.2 g fibre, 519 mg sodium

 Cook's Note: Queso fresco is a white, mild-flavoured Latin American cheese. It is often used to top spicy dishes, salads and soups. Look for it in the deli department of large grocery stores.

Fiesta Salad with Roasted Corn

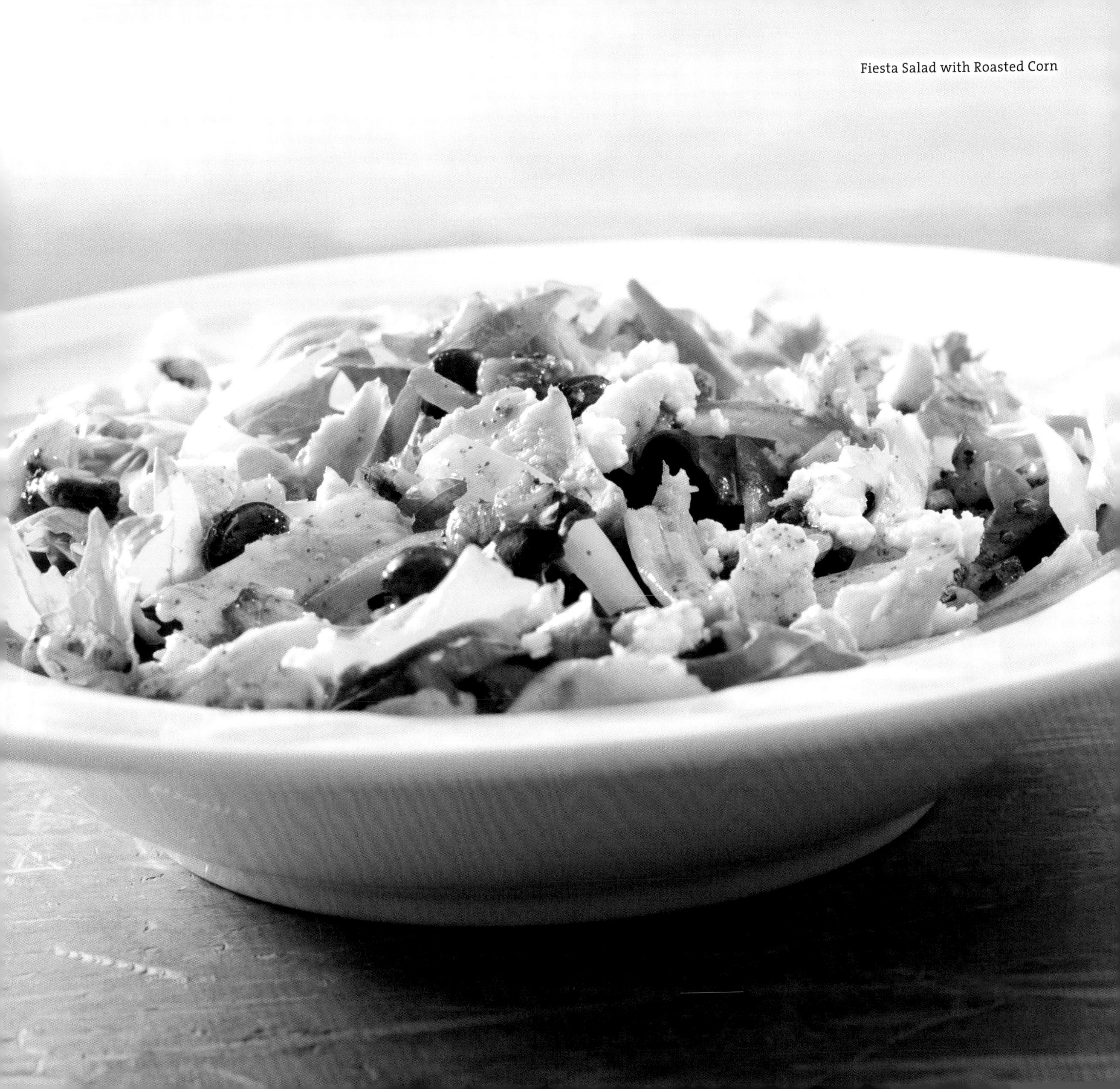

Ingredients:

¼ cup mayonnaise

2 tbsp balsamic vinegar

1 tbsp whole grain mustard

1 tsp liquid honey

8 cups thinly sliced cabbage (napa, savoy or green)

2 cups thinly sliced cored fennel bulb

¼ cup chopped fresh parsley

2 tbsp chopped fresh tarragon

Serves 8

Ingredients:

4 cups trimmed and cut green beans (1 inch)

2 tbsp white balsamic vinegar

1½ tsp liquid honey

1½ tsp whole grain mustard

¼ tsp freshly ground pepper

¼ cup extra-virgin olive oil

1 jar (375 mL) pickled cocktail onions, drained and halved (about 2 cups)

1 cup crumbled soft goat cheese, divided

1 cup julienned red bell pepper

½ cup unsalted shelled pumpkin seeds, toasted, divided

½ cup thinly sliced green onions

¼ cup chopped fresh parsley

Serves 8

Did You Know?

Shelled pumpkin seeds are also known as pepitas. They are dark green in colour and can be found in specialty food stores and the bulk foods section of most large grocery stores.

Fennel Coleslaw with Balsamic Dressing

1. To prepare dressing, combine mayonnaise, vinegar, mustard and honey until blended.

2. Combine cabbage, fennel, parsley and tarragon in a bowl.

3. Add dressing and toss to coat. Cover and refrigerate for 1 hour before serving. Toss before serving.

Nutritional analysis per serving:
82 calories, 5.7 g fat, 1.4 g protein, 7.5 g carbohydrate, 2.6 g fibre, 95 mg sodium

Green Bean and Pickled Onion Salad

1. Cook beans in boiling salted water until tender, about 3 minutes; drain.

2. Cool beans immediately in ice water; drain and set aside.

3. To prepare dressing, whisk together vinegar, honey, mustard and pepper until combined. Gradually whisk in oil until blended.

4. Combine beans, onions, ¾ cup cheese, red pepper, ⅓ cup pumpkin seeds, green onions and parsley in a bowl.

5. Add dressing and toss to combine. Top with remaining ¼ cup cheese and remaining 3 tbsp pumpkin seeds.

Nutritional analysis per serving:
232 calories, 17 g fat, 9.6 g protein, 12.9 g carbohydrate, 3 g fibre, 257 mg sodium

 Enjoy convenience, cost savings and instant heat with a natural gas fire pit. More benefits at atcogas.com.

Fried Fish Sandwiches

Sandwiches & Such

Fried Fish Sandwiches

Ingredients:

6 butter lettuce leaves

12 red onion slices

6 fried fish fillets from *Fish and Oven-Roasted Chips (recipe on page 71)*

6 hamburger buns

6 tbsp *Tartar Sauce (recipe on page 71)*

Makes 6

1. Place 1 lettuce leaf, 2 red onion slices and 1 fried fish fillet on each bottom half of buns. Top each fillet with 1 tbsp Tartar Sauce. Cover with top halves of buns.

Nutritional analysis per sandwich:
596 calories, 32.7 g fat, 32 g protein, 42.2 g carbohydrate, 2.1 g fibre, 796 mg sodium

Bean and Vegetable Quesadillas

Ingredients:

¾ cup refried beans

1 tsp chili powder

1 tsp garlic powder

1 tsp ground coriander

1 tsp freshly ground pepper

½ tsp salt

3 cups sliced quartered zucchini

2 cups chopped red onions

1 cup chopped orange bell pepper

2 tsp chili powder

2 tsp freshly ground pepper

1 tsp garlic powder

1 tsp ground coriander

1 tsp salt

2 tbsp canola oil

6 flour tortillas (10 inch)

1½ cups shredded Monterey Jack cheese

1 can (19 oz/540 mL) black beans, rinsed and drained

Salsa*

Sour cream*

Makes 6

1. Preheat oven to 350°F.

2. Combine refried beans, 1 tsp chili powder, 1 tsp garlic powder, 1 tsp coriander, 1 tsp pepper and ½ tsp salt; set aside.

3. Combine zucchini, red onions, orange pepper, 2 tsp chili powder, 2 tsp pepper, 1 tsp garlic powder, 1 tsp coriander and 1 tsp salt in a bowl; toss to coat vegetables with seasonings.

4. Heat oil in a large non-stick frypan over medium heat. Add vegetable mixture and sauté until softened, about 8 – 9 minutes. Remove from heat and set aside.

5. Spread refried bean mixture over each tortilla, dividing equally. Sprinkle ¼ cup cheese over each. Dividing equally, place vegetable mixture and black beans over half of each tortilla. Fold each tortilla in half and press down gently.

6. Transfer tortillas to a large parchment paper-lined rimmed baking sheet.

7. Bake until cheese is melted and filling is heated through, about 15 minutes.

8. Cut into wedges and serve with salsa and sour cream.

Nutritional analysis per quesadilla:
527 calories, 21 g fat, 21.2 g protein, 65.4 g carbohydrate, 11 g fibre, 1380 mg sodium

*Ingredient not included in nutritional analysis.

Shrimp and Avocado Tea Sandwiches

These small open-faced sandwiches are great served on a platter at an afternoon tea or at a party.

1. Cook shrimp in boiling water until pink and opaque; drain. Cool shrimp completely in ice water; drain.

2. Pat shrimp dry with paper towels. Remove tails from shrimp; discard tails. Dice shrimp. There should be about 1²/₃ cups.

3. Transfer shrimp to a bowl. Add avocado, oil, 2 tsp lemon juice, dill and ½ tsp salt; stir to combine and set aside.

4. Combine cream cheese, chives, lemon peel, 1 tsp lemon juice, ⅛ tsp salt and pepper until blended.

5. Spread cream cheese mixture on one side of bread slices, dividing equally.

6. Depending on size of bread slices, cut each in half or in thirds. Top pieces with shrimp mixture, dividing equally. Serve immediately or cover and refrigerate for up to 2 hours.

Nutritional analysis per tea sandwich:
49 calories, 3 g fat, 3.2 g protein, 2.1 g carbohydrate, 0.5 g fibre, 105 mg sodium

Ingredients:

¾ lb (0.375 kg) frozen peeled and deveined raw shrimp, thawed and rinsed

1 cup diced ripe avocado

2 tsp extra-virgin olive oil

2 tsp fresh lemon juice

1 tsp chopped fresh dill

½ tsp salt

²/₃ cup cream cheese, softened

2 tbsp thinly sliced fresh chives

1 tsp grated lemon peel

1 tsp fresh lemon juice

⅛ tsp salt

⅛ tsp freshly ground pepper

12 slices *Rye Bread (recipe on page 102)* or store-bought rye bread, ¼ inch thick

Makes about 30

Cook's Note: For a different presentation, 8 crustless white bread slices can be used instead of the rye bread slices. After being spread with the cream cheese mixture, cut each bread slice into 4 triangles and top each triangle with the shrimp mixture, dividing equally.

Ingredients:

½ cup salted butter, softened

¼ cup chopped fresh parsley

1½ tsp fresh lemon juice

1 clove garlic, finely chopped

12 slices *Everyday Bread (recipe on page 100)* or white bread

6 hard-cooked large eggs, peeled and sliced

2 tbsp *Chili Oil (recipe follows)*

1½ cups thinly sliced English cucumber

2 tsp coarse sea salt

Makes 18

Did You Know?

English cucumbers are longer than field cucumbers and have a sweeter flavour and fewer seeds. They are sometimes referred to as burpless cucumbers because they are supposedly easier to digest.

Ingredients:

¼ cup canola oil

1 tbsp red pepper flakes

1½ tsp cayenne pepper

1½ tsp chili powder

Egg and Cucumber Tea Sandwiches

These small rectangular sandwiches are a perfect thing to serve at a shower or luncheon.

1. Using medium speed of an electric mixer, beat together butter, parsley, lemon juice and garlic until smooth.

2. Spread butter mixture on one side of bread slices, dividing equally. Top each of 6 bread slices with 1 sliced egg. Dividing equally, drizzle eggs with Chili Oil and top with cucumber. Sprinkle cucumber with salt. Cover with remaining bread slices.

3. Press down firmly on each sandwich and wrap with plastic wrap. Refrigerate sandwiches for 30 minutes. This makes the sandwiches easier to cut.

4. Unwrap sandwiches and cut off crusts; reserve crusts for another use. Cut each sandwich crosswise into 3 equal finger sandwiches. Serve immediately or cover and refrigerate for up to 2 hours.

Nutritional analysis per tea sandwich:
119 calories, 8.8 g fat, 3.1 g protein, 6.7 g carbohydrate, 0.4 g fibre, 432 mg sodium

Chili Oil

This flavourful oil can be drizzled over sandwich fillings or soup servings to add some kick. It can also be used in place of canola oil to fry meat and vegetables.

1. Place all ingredients in a mini food processor; process for 30 seconds. Cover and refrigerate for 1 hour.

2. Strain oil mixture through a fine sieve into a bowl; discard solids.

3. May be refrigerated for up to 24 hours. Stir before using. Makes about 1/4 cup.

Nutritional analysis per 1 tbsp serving:
125 calories, 13.8 g fat, 0.2 g protein, 0.9 g carbohydrate, 0.5 g fibre, 7 mg sodium

Shrimp and Avocado Tea Sandwiches (page 49)
Crab Salad Baguette Bites (page 52)
Egg and Cucumber Tea Sandwiches

Brisket on a Bun

Ingredients:

1 tbsp canola oil

6 cups sliced onions

3 cups shredded *Pressure Cooker Beef Brisket (recipe on page 77)*

1 cup barbecue sauce

6 tbsp whole grain mustard

6 whole wheat hamburger buns

6 slices cheddar cheese or Monterey Jack cheese with jalapeno

Makes 6

1. Heat oil in a large non-stick frypan over medium heat. Add onions and cook, uncovered, stirring occasionally, until golden brown and reduced, about 17 minutes. Remove from heat.

2. Transfer onions to a heatproof bowl; cover and set aside.

3. Add Pressure Cooker Beef Brisket and barbecue sauce to same frypan; cook, stirring, over medium heat, until combined and heated through. Remove from heat.

4. Spread 1 tbsp mustard on each bottom half of buns. Dividing equally, top bottoms with brisket mixture, onions and cheese. Cover with top halves of buns.

Nutritional analysis per sandwich:
596 calories, 31.8 g fat, 29.8 g protein, 48.9 g carbohydrate, 5.9 g fibre, 1223 mg sodium

Crab Salad Baguette Bites

These baguette bites are a wonderful addition to a summer sandwich tray.

Ingredients:

1 lb (0.5 kg) cooked crabmeat, rinsed, squeezed dry and flaked

¼ cup mayonnaise

2 tbsp fresh lemon juice

2 tbsp tobiko (fish roe), optional

1 tbsp thinly sliced fresh chives

1 tsp grated lemon peel

½ tsp salt

½ tsp freshly ground pepper

2 tbsp salted butter, softened

16 baguette slices, ¼ inch thick

32 arugula leaves

Makes 16

1. Combine crabmeat, mayonnaise, lemon juice, tobiko, chives, lemon peel, salt and pepper; set aside.

2. Spread butter on one side of baguette slices, dividing equally. Top each with 2 arugula leaves and crabmeat mixture, dividing equally. Serve immediately or cover and refrigerate for up to 2 hours.

Nutritional analysis per baguette bite:
96 calories, 5 g fat, 7.2 g protein, 5.5 g carbohydrate, 0.3 g fibre, 409 mg sodium

Cook's Note: Check crabmeat carefully for any small pieces of shell and cartilage; remove and discard.

Tobiko is crunchy, bright, orange-red flying fish roe. Look for it in specialty fish stores or Asian grocery stores.

Ingredients:

12 thin slices pancetta

½ cup *Chipotle Mayo (recipe follows)*

8 slices *Everyday Bread (recipe on page 100)* or white bread, toasted

4 romaine lettuce leaves

12 Roma tomato slices

8 red onion slices

1 ripe avocado, sliced

Makes 4

Did You Know?

Pancetta is an Italian bacon that is available in the deli department of Italian grocery stores and most large grocery stores.

Ingredients:

1 cup mayonnaise

2 tbsp finely chopped canned chipotle peppers in adobo sauce

1 tbsp finely chopped fresh cilantro

1 tbsp thinly sliced green onion

Pancetta BLTs

This sandwich is a twist on the classic BLT. As a variation, toasted bagels can be used instead of bread.

1. Preheat oven to 400°F.

2. Place pancetta in a parchment paper-lined rimmed baking sheet.

3. Bake until pancetta is browned and crisp, about 15 minutes.

4. Spread 1 tbsp Chipotle Mayo on one side of each bread slice. Dividing equally, top each of 4 bread slices with lettuce, tomato, red onion, pancetta and avocado. Cover with remaining bread slices.

Nutritional analysis per sandwich:
532 calories, 38.9 g fat, 18.5 g protein, 33.3 g carbohydrate, 5.2 g fibre, 1570 mg sodium

Chipotle Mayo

1. Combine all ingredients until blended. May be refrigerated for up to 2 days.
   Makes about 1 cup.

Nutritional analysis per 1 tbsp serving:
100 calories, 11 g fat, 0.2 g protein, 0.7 g carbohydrate, 0.1 g fibre, 123 mg sodium

 With natural gas, your barbecue is always ready to grill. Find easy maintenance tips at atcogas.com.

Ingredients:

1 lb (0.5 kg) mild Italian sausage meat

¼ cup panko

1 large egg

2 cloves garlic, finely chopped

1 tsp basil, crumbled

1 tsp oregano, crumbled

½ tsp cayenne pepper

4 slices prosciutto

4 hamburger buns

4 slices provolone cheese

8 Roma tomato slices

¼ cup arugula

Basil Sour Cream (recipe follows)*

Makes 4

Ingredients:

½ cup sour cream

¼ cup chopped fresh basil

1 tbsp fresh lemon juice

1 tsp liquid honey

Italian Sausage Burgers

1. Combine sausage, panko, egg, garlic, basil, oregano and cayenne pepper until blended. Shape mixture into 4 patties. Cover and refrigerate for at least 1 hour or up to 2 hours.

2. Cook prosciutto in batches in a large non-stick frypan over medium heat until crisp, about 1 – 2 minutes per side.

3. Transfer prosciutto to a paper towel-lined plate.

4. Grill patties over medium heat on natural gas barbecue until completely cooked.

5. Serve in buns with prosciutto, cheese, tomato, arugula and Basil Sour Cream.

Nutritional analysis per burger:
578 calories, 34.7 g fat, 33.9 g protein, 31.6 g carbohydrate, 1.9 g fibre, 1738 mg sodium

*Ingredient not included in nutritional analysis.

Basil Sour Cream

1. Combine all ingredients until blended. Refrigerate until serving.
    Makes about 2/3 cup.

Nutritional analysis per 1 tbsp serving:
27 calories, 1.9 g fat, 0.4 g protein, 1.2 g carbohydrate, 0 g fibre, 6 mg sodium

 Safety Matters: Never use your range or any other natural gas appliance to heat your home. Doing so may put you and your family at risk of carbon monoxide poisoning. For more information, visit atcogas.com.

Grilled Ginger Pear Gouda Sandwiches

Ingredients:

8 slices smoked Gouda cheese

8 slices *Rye Bread (recipe on page 102)* or store-bought rye bread

½ cup *Ginger Pear Chutney (recipe follows)*

4 tsp salted butter, softened

Makes 4

1. Place 1 slice of cheese on each of 4 bread slices. Top each cheese-topped bread slice with 2 tbsp Ginger Pear Chutney, spreading evenly, and 1 additional slice of cheese. Cover with remaining bread slices.

2. Using 1 tsp butter for each sandwich, spread butter evenly over top and bottom of sandwich.

3. Grill sandwiches in batches in a large non-stick frypan over medium heat until sandwiches are golden brown and cheese is melted, about 3 minutes per side.

Nutritional analysis per sandwich:
432 calories, 21.9 g fat, 18.9 g protein, 39 g carbohydrate, 4.1 g fibre, 850 mg sodium

Ginger Pear Chutney

Ingredients:

1 tbsp salted butter

1 cup diced onion

3 firm ripe pears, peeled, cored and diced (about 3 cups)

1 tbsp grated fresh ginger

½ cup dry white wine

½ cup white wine vinegar

½ cup maple syrup

1 tbsp fresh lime juice

1. Melt butter in a medium non-reactive saucepan over medium heat. Add onion and sauté until softened, about 5 minutes.

2. Add pears and ginger; sauté until pears are softened, about 4 minutes.

3. Add wine and cook, stirring, until wine is almost evaporated. Stir in vinegar, maple syrup and lime juice. Bring to a boil.

4. Reduce heat and simmer, uncovered, stirring occasionally, until mixture is thickened, about 25 minutes. Remove from heat.

5. Transfer chutney to a heatproof bowl and cool to room temperature, stirring occasionally. May be refrigerated for up to 3 days. Makes about 2 cups.

Nutritional analysis per 1 tbsp serving:
31 calories, 0.4 g fat, 0.1 g protein, 6.3 g carbohydrate, 0.6 g fibre, 5 mg sodium

Steamed Pork Meatball Lettuce Wraps

Everyday Meals

Steamed Pork Meatball Lettuce Wraps

Ingredients:

Steamed Pork Meatballs (recipe follows)

½ cup hoisin sauce

20 butter lettuce leaves

20 fresh mint leaves

1¼ cups julienned carrots

1¼ cups julienned seeded English cucumber

¼ cup fresh cilantro leaves

Makes 10

1. Place hot Steamed Pork Meatballs in a heatproof bowl. Add hoisin sauce and toss to coat; set aside.

2. Make ten stacks of 2 lettuce leaves each. Dividing equally, top each lettuce stack with mint leaves, carrots and cucumber. Place 3 meatballs on top of vegetables on each lettuce stack. Garnish with cilantro. Wrap leaves around filling to enclose.

Nutritional analysis per wrap:
157 calories, 5 g fat, 20.2 g protein, 8.3 g carbohydrate, 1.1 g fibre, 561 mg sodium

Steamed Pork Meatballs

Ingredients:

2 lb (1 kg) lean ground pork

¼ cup oyster sauce

3 tbsp finely chopped shallot

4 tsp fish sauce

4 cloves garlic, finely chopped

1 tsp granulated sugar

1 tsp white pepper

 To learn how to make Steamed Pork Meatballs, visit our YouTube channel at youtube.com/TheBlueFlameKitchen

1. Combine all ingredients. Shape mixture into 30 balls, each measuring about 1½ inches; set aside.

2. To steam meatballs, use a saucepan with a tight-fitting lid and a heatproof steaming basket that will hold the meatballs above water in the saucepan. Bring water to a boil in saucepan.

3. Place only enough meatballs to form a single layer in the basket. Set basket over boiling water. Do not allow water to touch basket.

4. Cover and steam over boiling water until meatballs are completely cooked, about 10 – 15 minutes.

5. Repeat steaming procedure with remaining meatballs. Alternatively, meatballs may be placed on a rack in a parchment paper-lined rimmed baking sheet and baked in an oven at 350°F until completely cooked, about 20 minutes.
   Makes 30.

Nutritional analysis per meatball:
42 calories, 1.5 g fat, 6.4 g protein, 0.7 g carbohydrate, 0.1 g fibre, 128 mg sodium

Three Meat Bolognese Sauce

Bolognese sauce is a thick meat sauce that originates from Bologna in northern Italy. This version is made with ground beef, veal and pork. As the recipe makes a lot, the sauce can be frozen in usable portions. Serve it with your favourite pasta.

1. Tie rosemary, sage and thyme together with butcher's twine, forming a bundle; set aside.

2. Place onions, carrots and celery in a food processor; process until almost smooth.

3. Drain onion mixture in a fine sieve, pressing on onion mixture to remove excess moisture; set onion mixture aside.

4. Heat 1 tbsp oil in a non-reactive Dutch oven over medium heat. Add beef, pork and veal; cook, stirring to break up meat, until browned and cooked through. Add ½ tsp salt and ½ tsp pepper; stir to combine. Remove from heat.

5. Remove beef mixture with a slotted spoon; drain beef mixture on paper towels and set aside. Drain off excess fat from Dutch oven.

6. Melt butter with 2 tbsp oil in same Dutch oven over medium-low heat. Add onion mixture, herb bundle and bay leaf; sauté for 15 minutes.

7. Add tomatoes and stir to combine. Mash tomatoes with a potato masher. Return beef mixture to Dutch oven and stir to combine. Bring to a boil.

8. Reduce heat and simmer, uncovered, stirring occasionally, for 2 hours. Remove from heat; remove and discard herb bundle and bay leaf.

9. Stir in ½ tsp salt and ½ tsp pepper.

10. If not serving immediately, cool sauce quickly by placing Dutch oven in a sink of ice water and stirring sauce frequently to allow steam to escape. Do not allow ice water to enter Dutch oven.

11. If freezing, spoon cooled sauce into freezer containers and freeze for up to 2 months. Cooled sauce may also be spooned into containers and refrigerated for up to 2 days.

Nutritional analysis per ½ cup serving:
125 calories, 6.1 g fat, 9.4 g protein, 9 g carbohydrate, 1.8 g fibre, 487 mg sodium

Ingredients:

1 sprig fresh rosemary

1 sprig fresh sage

1 sprig fresh thyme

2½ cups chopped onions

2½ cups sliced carrots

1½ cups sliced celery

1 tbsp extra-virgin olive oil

1 lb (0.5 kg) lean ground beef

½ lb (0.25 kg) lean ground pork

½ lb (0.25 kg) ground veal

½ tsp salt

½ tsp freshly ground pepper

2 tbsp salted butter

2 tbsp extra-virgin olive oil

1 bay leaf

3 cans (28 oz/796 mL each) whole tomatoes

½ tsp salt

½ tsp freshly ground pepper

Makes about 10 1/2 cups

 Cook's Note: Ground veal is not readily available at regular grocery stores. Ask for it at specialty butcher shops. If desired, ground beef or pork may be used instead of ground veal.

Ingredients:

3 tbsp chili powder

1 tbsp paprika

1 tbsp canola oil

1½ tsp caraway seed

1 tsp dry mustard

1 tsp garlic powder

1 tsp ground allspice

¼ tsp cayenne pepper

1 lb (0.5 kg) boneless beef chuck steak,
    cut into 1 inch cubes

1 lb (0.5 kg) boneless pork shoulder roast,
    cut into 1 inch cubes

½ lb (0.25 kg) bison sirloin steak, cut into
    1 inch cubes

½ cup chopped bacon

2 cans (28 oz/796 mL each) whole tomatoes

2 cups chopped onions

1 can (5½ oz/156 mL) tomato paste

½ cup chopped carrot

½ cup chopped yellow bell pepper

¼ cup chopped celery

10 cloves garlic, finely chopped

1 tbsp thyme, crumbled

4 bay leaves

2 cans (19 oz/540 mL each) red kidney
    beans, rinsed and drained

3 tbsp packed golden brown sugar

1 tsp salt

1 tsp freshly ground pepper

Serves 10

Slow Cooker Range Chili

This chili contains beef, pork and bison, making it a great chili to serve to meat lovers.

1. Combine chili powder, paprika, oil, caraway seed, dry mustard, garlic powder, allspice and cayenne pepper in a large non-reactive bowl. Add beef, pork, bison and bacon; toss to coat meat with seasoning mixture. Add tomatoes, onions, tomato paste, carrot, yellow pepper, celery, garlic, thyme and bay leaves; stir to combine. May be prepared to this point, covered and refrigerated for up to 12 hours.

2. Transfer mixture to a 6 – 6½ quart slow cooker.

3. Cover and cook on high heat setting for 1 hour.

4. Reduce to low heat setting and continue cooking, covered, for 7 hours or until meat is tender.

5. Uncover slow cooker. Add beans, brown sugar, salt and pepper; stir gently to combine.

6. Cover and continue cooking on low heat setting until beans are heated through, about 15 minutes. Remove and discard bay leaves.

Nutritional analysis per serving:
467 calories, 21 g fat, 34.7 g protein, 37.7 g carbohydrate, 9.2 g fibre, 896 mg sodium

 Safety Matters: Natural gas flames are fire. Treat them with respect. Don't cook in loose clothing or spray flammable liquids nearby. For more safety tips, visit atcogas.com.

Ingredients:

1 tbsp canola oil

1⅔ cups diced onions

1 cup diced red bell pepper

1 cup diced yellow bell pepper

4 cloves garlic, finely chopped

1 cup no-salt-added chicken broth

1 lb (0.5 kg) boneless skinless
    chicken thighs

2 cups tomato sauce

1 tbsp chopped canned chipotle peppers
    in adobo sauce

1 can (19 oz/540 mL) black beans, rinsed
    and drained

½ cup frozen kernel corn

2 tbsp fresh lime juice

8 flour tortillas (10 inch)

1 cup shredded Monterey Jack cheese

Makes 8

Cook's Note: If desired, these enchiladas may be frozen before baking. Cool tomato sauce mixture and filling quickly and assemble enchiladas in a non-reactive metal baking pan; freeze. Bake enchiladas from frozen, covered, at 375°F until bubbly and heated through. Uncover and continue baking until lightly browned. As the enchiladas are baked from frozen, a metal baking pan must be used to ensure the pan does not break.

Chicken Enchiladas

1. Preheat oven to 350°F.

2. Heat oil in a non-reactive ovenproof Dutch oven over medium heat. Add onions, red pepper and yellow pepper; sauté for 3 minutes.

3. Add garlic and sauté for 2 minutes.

4. Add broth and cook, scraping to loosen browned bits. Add chicken, tomato sauce and chipotle peppers; stir to combine. Bring to a boil. Remove from heat.

5. Bake, covered, until chicken is tender and cooked through, about 30 – 40 minutes. Remove Dutch oven from oven.

6. Increase oven temperature to 375°F.

7. Meanwhile, using a slotted spoon, transfer chicken to a cutting board; set tomato sauce mixture aside. When cool enough to handle, use two forks to shred chicken.

8. To prepare filling, transfer shredded chicken to a bowl. Add beans, corn and lime juice; stir to combine.

9. Spread ½ cup tomato sauce mixture in bottom of a greased 9x13 inch baking dish.

10. Spoon about ½ cup filling down centre of each tortilla. Roll up tortillas to enclose filling and place, seam side down, in a single layer on top of tomato sauce mixture in baking dish. Pour remaining tomato sauce mixture over top. Sprinkle with cheese.

11. Bake, covered, until bubbly and heated through, about 30 minutes.

12. Uncover and continue baking until lightly browned, about 10 minutes.

Nutritional analysis per enchilada:
434 calories, 13.6 g fat, 22.1 g protein, 57 g carbohydrate, 7.9 g fibre, 966 mg sodium

Buttermilk Biscuits with White Sausage Gravy

1. Heat oil in a large saucepan over medium heat. Add sausage and cook, stirring to break up sausage, until browned and cooked through. Remove from heat.

2. Remove sausage with a slotted spoon; drain sausage on paper towels and set aside. Do not drain off excess fat from saucepan.

3. Return saucepan to medium heat. Add onion and sauté until softened, about 2 minutes. Add garlic and sauté for 2 minutes.

4. Whisk in flour and cook, stirring, for 1 minute. Add milk, ½ cup at a time, cooking and whisking constantly until smooth. Bring to a boil, whisking frequently.

5. Reduce heat and simmer, whisking frequently, until thickened, about 4 – 5 minutes.

6. Return sausage to saucepan. Add thyme and dry mustard; cook, stirring, until combined and sausage is heated through. Season to taste with pepper.

7. Serve immediately over Buttermilk Biscuits.

Nutritional analysis per serving:
546 calories, 40.6 g fat, 26.3 g protein, 17.8 g carbohydrate, 0.8 g fibre, 883 mg sodium
*Ingredient not included in nutritional analysis.

Ingredients:

1 tbsp canola oil

1 lb (0.5 kg) pork sausages, casings removed or pork sausage meat

½ cup finely chopped onion

4 cloves garlic, finely chopped

¼ cup all-purpose flour

3 cups milk (2%)

1 tbsp chopped fresh thyme

1 tsp dry mustard

Freshly ground pepper*

Buttermilk Biscuits (recipe follows)

Serves 4

Did You Know?

Biscuits and gravy is a breakfast dish that is common in the southern United States. The cream-coloured gravy, typically made from pork sausage, flour and milk, is poured over biscuits on a plate. Try our version as a comforting main dish.

Buttermilk Biscuits

1. Preheat oven to 425°F.

2. Combine flour, baking powder, thyme, sage, baking soda and salt in a bowl. Cut in butter with a pastry blender until mixture resembles coarse meal. Add buttermilk and stir just until combined.

3. Turn dough out onto a lightly floured surface. Knead dough gently and pat dough into a circle about ¾ inch thick. Using a floured 2¼ inch cookie cutter, cut dough into rounds. Place rounds on a lightly greased rimmed baking sheet.

4. Bake for 10 – 12 minutes or until light golden. Makes about 12.

Nutritional analysis per biscuit:
140 calories, 6.6 g fat, 2.9 g protein, 17.2 g carbohydrate, 0.6 g fibre, 238 mg sodium

Ingredients:

2 cups all-purpose flour

1 tbsp baking powder

½ tsp thyme, crumbled

¼ tsp sage, crumbled

¼ tsp baking soda

¼ tsp salt

6 tbsp salted butter, chilled and cubed

1 cup buttermilk

Ingredients:

4 cups buttermilk*

½ cup chopped shallots*

4 cloves garlic, bruised*

3 sprigs fresh thyme*

2 bay leaves*

1½ tsp chili powder*

1½ tsp dry mustard*

1½ tsp ground cumin*

½ tsp cayenne pepper*

1 whole fryer chicken (about 3½ lb/1.75 kg),
    cut into 9 pieces (2 breasts, 2 drumsticks,
    2 thighs, 2 wings and 1 back)

2 cups all-purpose flour

1 tbsp baking powder

2½ tsp salt

1 tsp dry mustard

1 tsp garlic powder

1 tsp freshly ground pepper

½ tsp celery seed

½ tsp paprika

Canola oil

Salt*

Makes 9 pieces

Did You Know?

A fryer chicken, also referred to as a broiler
chicken or a broiler-fryer, is a young, small
chicken. It is best when cut up or butterflied
and cooked using a high heat method such as
broiling, frying or grilling. A fryer chicken can
also be roasted whole.

Buttermilk-Marinated Fried Chicken

1. To prepare marinade, combine buttermilk, shallots, garlic, thyme, bay leaves, chili powder, 1½ tsp dry mustard, cumin and cayenne pepper.

2. Divide marinade between two large heavy zip-lock plastic bags. Add 5 chicken pieces to one bag and 4 to the other bag; squeeze bags to coat chicken with marinade. Seal bags and place on a tray. Refrigerate, turning bags occasionally, for at least 8 hours or up to 24 hours.

3. To prepare coating, combine flour, baking powder, salt, 1 tsp dry mustard, garlic powder, pepper, celery seed and paprika in a large shallow bowl.

4. Remove chicken from marinade; discard marinade.

5. Working with one piece at a time, toss chicken in coating, patting so that coating adheres; shake off excess coating.

6. Heat 3½ inches oil to 325°F in a stockpot over medium-high heat.

7. Working in batches, carefully place chicken in oil; fry until chicken is cooked through and coating is golden brown, about 12 – 14 minutes for white meat pieces and 15 – 17 minutes for dark meat pieces.

8. Remove chicken with a slotted spoon; drain chicken on paper towels. Sprinkle lightly with additional salt. Serve immediately.

Nutritional analysis per piece:
604 calories, 46.8 g fat, 23 g protein, 22.1 g carbohydrate, 0.9 g fibre, 843 mg sodium

*Ingredient not included in nutritional analysis.

 Cook's Note: If desired, 3½ lb (1.75 kg) of any bone-in chicken pieces with skin may be used instead of the whole fryer chicken cut up.

Ingredients:

10 Brussels sprouts

3 cups rotini pasta or other short pasta

1½ cups coarsely chopped bacon
   or pancetta

2 tbsp salted butter

2 tbsp extra-virgin olive oil

3½ cups diced mushrooms

1 cup diced shallots

4 cloves garlic, finely chopped

¼ tsp salt

1 cup dry white wine

1 cup whipping cream

¼ cup freshly grated Parmesan cheese

1 tbsp fresh lemon juice

2 tsp grated lemon peel

Freshly grated Parmesan cheese*

Serves 4

Mushroom Cream Pasta with Brussels Sprouts

1. Cut off ends of Brussels sprouts; discard ends. Separate Brussels sprouts into leaves; discard cores. There should be about 2 cups leaves; set aside.

2. Cook pasta according to package directions; drain and set aside.

3. Sauté bacon in a large deep non-stick frypan over medium heat until browned and crisp. Remove from heat.

4. Remove bacon with a slotted spoon; drain bacon on paper towels and set aside. Drain off excess fat from frypan.

5. Melt butter with oil in same frypan over medium heat. Add mushrooms and sauté until softened and lightly browned, about 2 – 3 minutes.

6. Add shallots, garlic and salt; sauté until shallots are softened, about 3 minutes.

7. Increase heat to medium-high. Return bacon to frypan. Add Brussels sprouts leaves and sauté for 30 seconds.

8. Add wine and cook, stirring, for 1 minute.

9. Add cream and stir to combine. Bring to a simmer and cook, stirring, until cream mixture is slightly reduced, about 3 minutes.

10. Add ¼ cup Parmesan cheese, lemon juice and lemon peel; stir to combine. Add pasta and toss to combine; cook, stirring, until pasta is heated through.

11. Serve topped with additional Parmesan cheese.

Nutritional analysis per serving:
973 calories, 61.3 g fat, 36.5 g protein, 60.3 g carbohydrate, 5.5 g fibre, 1641 mg sodium

*Ingredient not included in nutritional analysis.

Mushroom Cream Pasta with Brussels Sprouts

Ingredients:

1 cup canola oil*

¼ cup fresh lemon juice*

1 small onion, cut into chunks*

4 bay leaves*

4 sprigs fresh thyme*

3 sprigs fresh mint*

8 bone-in chicken thighs with skin

¼ tsp salt

¼ tsp freshly ground pepper

Serves 4

Did You Know?

Lemons release more juice if at room temperature. To get the most juice, apply moderate pressure with the palm of your hand and roll the lemon back and forth on a countertop. Cut the lemon in half crosswise and ream out the juice using a reamer or juicer. If a reamer or juicer is not available, use a fork to obtain the juice.

Lemon Herb Marinated Chicken

1. To prepare marinade, combine oil, lemon juice, onion, bay leaves, thyme and mint in a large heavy zip-lock plastic bag.

2. Add chicken and squeeze bag to coat chicken with marinade. Seal bag and place on a plate. Refrigerate, turning bag occasionally, for 4 hours.

3. Remove plate with bag from refrigerator and let stand for 30 minutes.

4. Remove chicken from marinade; discard marinade, onion, bay leaves, thyme and mint. Sprinkle chicken with salt and pepper.

5. Brown chicken on both sides in a large non-stick frypan over medium heat, about 3 minutes per side.

6. Reduce heat to low and cook until chicken is cooked through, about 30 – 35 minutes. Alternatively, chicken may be grilled over low heat on natural gas barbecue until chicken is cooked through.

Nutritional analysis per serving:
397 calories, 28.7 g fat, 32.5 g protein, 0.1 g carbohydrate, 0 g fibre, 288 mg sodium

*Ingredient not included in nutritional analysis.

 Transform your garage into a year-round shop or hobby area with a natural gas garage heater. Find out more at atcogas.com.

Fish and Oven-Roasted Chips

This is a spin on a British classic – fish and chips. Instead of fries, roasted potato wedges are the chips in this recipe. For something different, use the fried fish and tartar sauce in our Fried Fish Sandwiches (recipe on page 48).

1. Preheat oven to 425°F.

2. To prepare roasted potatoes, cut each potato lengthwise into 8 wedges. There should be about 7 cups.

3. Combine potatoes, 1 tbsp oil and sea salt in a bowl; toss to coat.

4. Place potatoes in a single layer in a greased or non-stick foil-lined large rimmed baking sheet.

5. Bake, stirring occasionally, until potatoes are tender and lightly browned, about 40 – 50 minutes.

6. Meanwhile, combine flour, salt and pepper in a pie plate. Whisk together milk and egg in a second pie plate until blended. Place panko in a third pie plate.

7. Working with one piece at a time, dredge fish in flour mixture, shaking off excess. Dip fish in milk mixture, turning to coat both sides. Place fish in panko, pressing lightly so that panko adheres; turn to coat both sides.

8. Heat 1 cup oil in a 10 inch frypan over medium-high heat. Working in batches, carefully place fish in oil; fry until fish flakes easily with a fork and coating is golden brown, about 2 – 3 minutes per side.

9. Remove fish with a slotted spoon; drain fish on paper towels. Discard leftover oil.

10. Serve fish with Tartar Sauce and roasted potatoes.

Nutritional analysis per serving:
533 calories, 24.4 g fat, 31.3 g protein, 46.4 g carbohydrate, 3.8 g fibre, 881 mg sodium

*Ingredient not included in nutritional analysis.

Ingredients:

6 unpeeled medium yellow potatoes

1 tbsp canola oil

1 tsp coarse sea salt

½ cup all-purpose flour

1 tsp salt

½ tsp freshly ground pepper

½ cup milk (2%)

1 large egg

1 cup panko

6 halibut fillets or other firm-fleshed white fish fillets (about 4 oz/125 g each)

1 cup canola oil

*Tartar Sauce (recipe follows)**

Serves 6

 To learn how to shallow fry fish, visit our YouTube channel at youtube.com/TheBlueFlameKitchen

Tartar Sauce

1. Combine all ingredients until blended. May be refrigerated for up to 2 days. Makes about 2/3 cup.

Nutritional analysis per 1 tbsp serving:
81 calories, 8.8 g fat, 0.2 g protein, 0.9 g carbohydrate, 0.1 g fibre, 107 mg sodium

Ingredients:

½ cup mayonnaise

1 tbsp chopped gherkins or other pickles

1 tbsp chopped shallot

1 tbsp drained capers, chopped

2 tsp grated lemon peel

1 tsp fresh lemon juice

Ingredients:

½ cup liquid honey

2 tbsp Dijon mustard

1½ tbsp fresh lemon juice

1 tsp chopped fresh rosemary

½ tsp salt

¼ tsp freshly ground pepper

1 pork tenderloin (1 lb/0.5 kg)

Serves 4

Honey-Glazed Pork Tenderloin

1. Preheat oven to 425°F.

2. To prepare glaze, combine all ingredients except pork in a small non-reactive saucepan. Bring to a simmer over medium heat and cook, whisking frequently, for 3 minutes. Remove from heat.

3. Reserve ¼ cup of glaze to serve with pork; remaining glaze will be used to brush pork during cooking.

4. Place pork in a non-stick foil-lined rimmed baking sheet. Brush pork with half of remaining glaze, rotating to brush all sides.

5. Bake, uncovered, for 10 minutes. Remove pork from oven.

6. Reduce oven temperature to 350°F. Brush pork with rest of remaining glaze, rotating to brush all sides.

7. Continue baking, uncovered, until a meat thermometer registers 160°F, about 20 – 25 minutes.

8. Let stand for 10 minutes before slicing.

9. Meanwhile, reheat the ¼ cup of reserved glaze.

10. Slice pork and serve drizzled with reserved glaze.

Nutritional analysis per serving:
288 calories, 4.7 g fat, 26.3 g protein, 36.6 g carbohydrate, 0.4 g fibre, 539 mg sodium

 Cook's Note: As an alternative to using the oven, pork may be grilled. Reserve ¼ cup of glaze to serve with pork; remaining glaze will be used to brush pork during grilling. Sear pork on all sides over medium-high heat on natural gas barbecue. Brush pork with half of remaining glaze, rotating to brush all sides. Grill over low heat until a meat thermometer registers 160°F, brushing pork with rest of remaining glaze during last 10 – 15 minutes of grilling. Let stand for 10 minutes before slicing. Reheat the ¼ cup of reserved glaze to drizzle over sliced pork.

Ingredients:

3 tbsp Thai yellow curry paste

3 tbsp peanut oil, divided

2 tsp salt

12 boneless skinless chicken thighs

3 whole star anise

2 cinnamon sticks (3 inch)

½ tsp ground cardamom

¾ cup quartered shallots

2 cups no-salt-added chicken broth

2 tbsp fish sauce

2 cups cubed peeled yellow
    potatoes (1 inch)

1 can (400 mL) coconut milk

1 cup fresh basil leaves, divided

¼ cup unsalted blanched roasted peanuts,
    chopped

2 tbsp packed golden brown sugar

1 tbsp tamarind paste or fresh lime juice

Hot cooked rice*

Serves 6

Did You Know?

Thai yellow curry paste should be available
at Asian grocery stores. If desired, it may be
substituted with Thai red or green curry paste.
Look for them in the Asian section of large
grocery stores.

 To learn how to make Thai Chicken
Curry, visit our YouTube channel at
youtube.com/TheBlueFlameKitchen

Thai Chicken Curry

1. Combine curry paste, 1 tbsp oil and salt in a bowl. Add chicken and toss to coat. Let stand for 10 minutes.

2. Meanwhile, heat remaining 2 tbsp oil in a Dutch oven over medium heat. Add star anise, cinnamon sticks and cardamom; cook, stirring, until fragrant, about 1 minute.

3. Add shallots and sauté until softened and lightly browned, about 2 minutes.

4. Transfer shallots to a plate.

5. Add chicken to Dutch oven and brown on both sides.

6. Return shallots to Dutch oven. Add broth and fish sauce; stir to combine. Bring to a boil.

7. Reduce heat and simmer, covered, stirring occasionally, for 1 hour.

8. Add potatoes, coconut milk and ½ cup basil; stir to combine. Bring to a simmer and cook, covered, stirring occasionally, until chicken and potatoes are tender, about 20 – 25 minutes. Remove from heat; remove and discard star anise and cinnamon sticks.

9. Stir in remaining ½ cup basil, peanuts, brown sugar and tamarind paste.

10. Serve over rice.

Nutritional analysis per serving:
489 calories, 29 g fat, 34 g protein, 25.7 g carbohydrate, 3.2 g fibre, 1700 mg sodium

*Ingredient not included in nutritional analysis.

 Cook's Note: Tamarind paste is made from the fruit of a tree that is native to Asia and northern Africa and also found in India. Look for tamarind paste in Asian or Indian grocery stores.

Thai Chicken Curry

Ingredients:

1 tbsp canola oil

1 cup diced onion

1 cup diced red bell pepper

2 cloves garlic, finely chopped

1 tsp chili powder

1 tsp ground cumin

1 tsp smoked paprika

1 lb (0.5 kg) ground turkey

1 can (19 oz/540 mL) black beans,
rinsed and drained

2 cups cooked quinoa, cooled

2 cups medium salsa, divided

1½ cups shredded Monterey Jack
cheese, divided

1 cup frozen kernel corn

2 large eggs, lightly beaten

2 tbsp chopped fresh cilantro

1 tsp grated lime peel

⅛ tsp cayenne pepper

⅛ tsp salt

Makes about 20

Did You Know?

Smoked paprika is made from Spanish red peppers that are dried and smoked over wood planks. This gives smoked paprika its characteristic smoky flavour. If unavailable, regular paprika may be used.

Turkey and Quinoa Mini Meat Loaves

1. Preheat oven to 375°F.

2. Heat oil in a medium non-stick frypan over medium heat. Add onion and red pepper; sauté until softened, about 3 – 4 minutes.

3. Add garlic, chili powder, cumin and paprika; cook, stirring, for 1 minute. Remove from heat and cool to room temperature.

4. Combine onion mixture, turkey, beans, quinoa, 1 cup salsa, 1 cup cheese, corn, beaten eggs, cilantro, lime peel, cayenne pepper and salt until blended.

5. Spoon mixture into greased muffin cups. Dividing equally, top mixture in each muffin cup with remaining 1 cup salsa and remaining ½ cup cheese.

6. Bake until meat loaves are lightly browned on top and a meat thermometer inserted in centres registers 175°F, about 35 – 40 minutes.

7. Let stand for 5 minutes before serving.

Nutritional analysis per mini meat loaf:
145 calories, 6.5 g fat, 10.2 g protein, 12.1 g carbohydrate, 2.8 g fibre, 257 mg sodium

 Cook's Note: Quinoa should be thoroughly rinsed and drained, then cooked using a ratio of one part quinoa to two parts water. Bring water to a boil in a saucepan. Stir in quinoa and return to a boil. Reduce heat and simmer, covered, until liquid is absorbed and quinoa is tender. Fluff quinoa with a fork. Cooking ¾ cup quinoa should yield more than enough cooked quinoa for this recipe.

Pressure Cooker Beef Brisket

Brisket is a cut of beef that is usually cooked at a low heat for a lengthy period of time in order to tenderize the meat and develop flavour. Using a pressure cooker helps achieve these results in less time. The meat in this recipe can be enjoyed on its own or used in our Brisket Hash (recipe on page 10) and our Brisket on a Bun (recipe on page 52).

1. Sprinkle brisket with salt and pepper.

2. Heat oil in a 6 quart pressure cooker over medium-high heat. Add brisket in batches and brown on all sides.

3. Transfer brisket to a plate; set aside.

4. Add wine to pressure cooker and cook, stirring, until wine is reduced by half. Add onions, celery, broth, garlic, bay leaves and rosemary; stir to combine.

5. Return brisket and any accumulated juices to pressure cooker. Cover with lid and lock it in place. Bring to high pressure over high heat.

6. Cook for 1 hour, adjusting heat as needed to maintain high pressure.

7. Carefully remove from heat and allow steam to release naturally. This may take 15 minutes.

8. Wearing oven mitts, carefully open lid away from yourself to protect from steam.

9. Transfer brisket to a cutting board; discard onion mixture or reserve for another use. When cool enough to handle, use two forks to shred brisket. There should be about 8 cups.

Nutritional analysis per serving:
378 calories, 28.9 g fat, 27.5 g protein, 0.1 g carbohydrate, 0 g fibre, 358 mg sodium

*Ingredient not included in nutritional analysis.

Ingredients:

4 lb (2 kg) boneless beef brisket, cut into 6 pieces

½ tsp salt

½ tsp freshly ground pepper

2 tbsp canola oil

½ cup dry red wine*

4 cups chopped onions (1 inch)*

2 cups chopped celery (1 inch)*

1 cup no-salt-added beef broth*

6 cloves garlic*

4 bay leaves*

1 sprig fresh rosemary or 1 tsp dried rosemary, crumbled*

Serves 10

Did You Know?

A pressure cooker is a pot with a special locking lid that allows foods to be cooked quickly at a high temperature under steam pressure. It is ideal for cooking soups, stews and tougher cuts of meat. Look for pressure cookers in department stores and specialty kitchen stores.

Most pressure cookers are designed to be used on the stove-top. As pressure cookers vary, always use them according to the manufacturer's instructions.

 Cook's Note: Beef brisket may not be readily available at regular grocery stores. Ask your store's butcher about availability or look for it at specialty butcher shops.

Ingredients:

1 tbsp chili powder

1 tsp garlic powder

1 tsp ground coriander

1 tsp ground cumin

1 tsp onion powder

1 tsp salt

1 tsp freshly ground pepper

1 lb (0.5 kg) frozen peeled and deveined raw shrimp, thawed and rinsed

1 cup chopped bacon

2 tbsp fresh lemon juice

1 tbsp salted butter

Cheesy Grits (recipe follows)*

Serves 4

Shrimp and Cheesy Grits

The term grits is used to describe a ground corn product that is cooked and often eaten at breakfast in the southern United States. Shrimp and grits is a popular dish in many of those states. This version is served as an entree, but could also be served as a side dish.

1. Combine chili powder, garlic powder, coriander, cumin, onion powder, salt and pepper in a bowl. Add shrimp and toss to coat. Cover and let stand for 30 minutes.

2. Meanwhile, sauté bacon in a large non-stick frypan over medium heat until browned and crisp. Remove from heat.

3. Remove bacon with a slotted spoon; drain bacon on paper towels and set aside. Drain off all but 2 tbsp fat from frypan.

4. Return frypan to medium heat. Add shrimp and cook, stirring frequently, until shrimp are pink and opaque, about 3 – 4 minutes. Do not overcook.

5. Turn heat off. Add lemon juice and butter, stirring until butter is melted. Return bacon to frypan and stir to combine.

6. Serve shrimp mixture immediately over Cheesy Grits.

Nutritional analysis per serving:
260 calories, 16.6 g fat, 22.6 g protein, 4.5 g carbohydrate, 1 g fibre, 1656 mg sodium

*Ingredient not included in nutritional analysis.

Ingredients:

1 tbsp canola oil

½ cup diced onion

3 cups no-salt-added chicken broth

2½ cups milk (2%)

1½ cups cornmeal

2 cups shredded cheddar or Monterey Jack cheese

¼ cup fresh lemon juice

2 tbsp salted butter

2 tbsp chopped fresh parsley

Cheesy Grits

1. Heat oil in a large saucepan over medium heat. Add onion and sauté until softened, about 3 – 4 minutes.

2. Add broth and milk; stir to combine. Bring to a boil over medium heat, stirring frequently.

3. Reduce heat to a simmer and gradually whisk in cornmeal; cook, stirring, until liquid is absorbed and cornmeal is softened. Remove from heat.

4. Add cheese, lemon juice, butter and parsley, stirring until cheese and butter are melted. Serve immediately. Makes about 6 1/2 cups.

Nutritional analysis per ½ cup serving:
176 calories, 9.9 g fat, 8.2 g protein, 14.1 g carbohydrate, 1.2 g fibre, 167 mg sodium

Ricotta Gnocchi

Sides

Ingredients:

1 cup ricotta cheese

½ cup freshly grated Parmesan cheese

2 large eggs

⅛ tsp salt

⅛ tsp freshly ground pepper

1⅓ cups all-purpose flour, divided

Serves 8

Did You Know?

Ricotta cheese is a fresh, soft, moist white cheese. It is slightly grainy with a texture similar to fine cottage cheese. Ricotta cheese is sold in tubs and is most often used in Italian dishes such as cannelloni and lasagna, as well as in desserts such as cheesecake.

 To learn how to make Ricotta Gnocchi, visit our YouTube channel at youtube.com/TheBlueFlameKitchen

Ricotta Gnocchi

Gnocchi are small Italian dumplings that are often served as a side dish. Serve this version with our Three Meat Bolognese Sauce (recipe on page 61), our Kale Pesto (recipe on page 86) or your favourite sauce.

1. Stir together ricotta cheese, Parmesan cheese, eggs, salt and pepper in a bowl until blended.

2. Stir in 1 cup flour until dough comes together; gradually stir in remaining ⅓ cup flour, 1 tbsp at a time, if dough is too sticky.

3. Turn dough out onto a well-floured surface. Knead dough for 3 minutes.

4. Dust dough with flour and divide dough into four pieces. On a lightly floured surface, roll each piece into a rope ½ inch in diameter. Cut each rope into ½ inch pieces.

5. Gnocchi may be prepared to this point and frozen. If freezing, place gnocchi in a single layer on a lightly floured tray; cover and freeze. Once gnocchi are frozen, transfer gnocchi to an airtight container and freeze for up to 1 month. Do not thaw before cooking.

6. Cook gnocchi in batches in boiling salted water until gnocchi float to surface and are tender, about 1 – 2 minutes if fresh and 3 – 4 minutes if frozen.

7. Remove gnocchi with a slotted spoon and transfer to a serving dish.

8. Serve immediately with a sauce.

Nutritional analysis per serving:
165 calories, 6.5 g fat, 8.8 g protein, 17.1 g carbohydrate, 0.6 g fibre, 154 mg sodium

 Safety Matters: If you have continual difficulty getting one or more natural gas burners lit, contact a qualified technician to have the unit serviced. For more safety tips, visit atcogas.com.

Collard Greens

1. Heat oil in a medium non-reactive saucepan over medium heat. Add onion and sauté until softened, about 5 minutes.

2. Add garlic and sauté for 1 minute.

3. Add collard greens and cook, stirring, until collard greens start to wilt. Add broth and cook, uncovered, stirring occasionally, until most of liquid is evaporated, about 10 minutes. Remove from heat.

4. Add tomatoes, lemon juice, lemon peel, salt and pepper; stir to combine. Serve immediately.

Nutritional analysis per serving:
66 calories, 3.7 g fat, 1.7 g protein, 7.7 g carbohydrate, 2.6 g fibre, 303 mg sodium

 Cook's Note: Collard greens are a type of cabbage, but they do not grow as a head. They are often cooked and eaten as a side dish in the southern United States. They have a flavour that is similar to both kale and cabbage. Look for collard greens in the organic produce section of large grocery stores.

Ingredients:

1 tbsp extra-virgin olive oil

½ cup diced onion

2 cloves garlic, finely chopped

4 cups chopped trimmed collard greens

1 cup no-salt-added vegetable broth or water

1 cup diced seeded Roma tomatoes

2 tbsp fresh lemon juice

1 tsp grated lemon peel

½ tsp salt

½ tsp freshly ground pepper

Serves 4

Zesty Creamed Peas

1. Cook peas in boiling water until tender; drain and set aside.

2. Heat milk over low heat; keep warm.

3. Melt butter in a medium saucepan over medium-low heat. Add flour and cook, stirring, for 3 minutes.

4. Add heated milk, ½ cup at a time, cooking and stirring constantly until smooth. Add salt, pepper, cayenne pepper and nutmeg; stir to combine.

5. Reduce heat to low and cook, stirring frequently, until thickened, about 15 minutes.

6. Add peas and lemon peel; cook, stirring, until combined and peas are heated through. Serve immediately.

Nutritional analysis per serving:
169 calories, 8.1 g fat, 7.4 g protein, 17.3 g carbohydrate, 3.3 g fibre, 559 mg sodium

Ingredients:

3 cups fresh or frozen green peas

2½ cups milk (2%)

3 tbsp salted butter

3 tbsp all-purpose flour

1 tsp salt

¼ tsp freshly ground pepper

⅛ tsp cayenne pepper

⅛ tsp nutmeg

1 tbsp grated lemon peel

Serves 6

Ingredients:

⅓ cup extra-virgin olive oil

2½ tbsp balsamic vinegar

1 tbsp Dijon mustard

20 asparagus spears, trimmed

Serves 4

Did You Know?

Before preparing asparagus, you should hold each stalk with two hands and gently bend at its bottom. Asparagus will snap where it is woody; discard bottom ends.

Ingredients:

1 tsp salted butter

1 tbsp canola oil

1 cup sliced leeks (white and tender light green portions only)

1 clove garlic, finely chopped

4 cups no-salt-added chicken broth

1 cup cornmeal

1 cup shredded Gouda cheese

1 tbsp chopped fresh basil or 1 tsp dried basil, crumbled

¾ tsp freshly ground pepper

½ tsp salt

Serves 6

 To learn how to make Leek and Gouda Polenta, visit our YouTube channel at youtube.com/TheBlueFlameKitchen

Balsamic Grilled Asparagus

1. To prepare marinade, combine all ingredients except asparagus in a large heavy zip-lock plastic bag.

2. Add asparagus and squeeze bag to coat asparagus with marinade. Seal bag and place on a plate. Refrigerate, turning bag occasionally, for 1 hour.

3. Remove asparagus from marinade; discard marinade.

4. Grill asparagus over medium heat on natural gas barbecue, turning occasionally, until tender, about 5 – 7 minutes.

Nutritional analysis per serving:
97 calories, 8.6 g fat, 1.9 g protein, 4.2 g carbohydrate, 1.7 g fibre, 48 mg sodium

Leek and Gouda Polenta

1. Melt butter with oil in a large saucepan over medium heat. Add leeks and sauté until softened, about 4 – 5 minutes.

2. Add garlic and sauté for 1 minute.

3. Add broth and stir to combine. Bring to a boil over medium heat.

4. Reduce heat to a simmer and gradually whisk in cornmeal; cook, stirring, until liquid is absorbed and cornmeal is softened. Remove from heat.

5. Add cheese, basil, pepper and salt, stirring until cheese is melted. Serve immediately.

Nutritional analysis per serving:
201 calories, 10 g fat, 10 g protein, 18.5 g carbohydrate, 1.9 g fibre, 451 mg sodium

 Cook's Note: Cornmeal is made by grinding dried corn kernels into a fine, medium or coarse meal. Most cornmeal sold in our grocery stores is finely ground.

Sugar and Spice Carrots

Ingredients:

3 tbsp salted butter, divided

1½ lb small garden carrots, trimmed

1 tsp ground ancho chile pepper

½ tsp cinnamon

¼ tsp nutmeg

¼ tsp salt

⅛ tsp freshly ground pepper

¼ cup packed golden brown sugar

¼ cup water

2 tbsp fresh lemon juice

1 tsp grated lemon peel

Serves 6

1. Melt 1½ tbsp butter in a large deep non-stick frypan over medium heat. Add carrots, ancho chile pepper, cinnamon, nutmeg, salt and pepper; cook, stirring, for 4 minutes.

2. Add brown sugar, water, lemon juice and lemon peel; stir to combine. Bring to a boil.

3. Reduce heat and simmer, covered, stirring occasionally, until carrots are tender crisp, about 7 – 8 minutes.

4. Uncover and add remaining 1½ tbsp butter; cook, stirring frequently, until butter is melted and carrots are tender and glazed, about 2 minutes. Serve immediately.

Nutritional analysis per serving:
138 calories, 6.1 g fat, 1.3 g protein, 21.4 g carbohydrate, 3.6 g fibre, 236 mg sodium

 Cook's Note: If desired, 6 cups carrots sticks (3 inch) may be used instead of small garden carrots.

 To learn how to cook garden carrots, visit our YouTube channel at youtube.com/TheBlueFlameKitchen

Horseradish Mashed Potatoes

Ingredients:

2 lb yellow potatoes, peeled and cut into 1 inch chunks

¾ cup buttermilk

½ cup salted butter

¼ cup prepared horseradish

½ tsp salt

½ tsp freshly ground pepper

Serves 6

1. Cook potatoes in boiling salted water until tender.

2. Meanwhile, place buttermilk and butter in a small saucepan over low heat; cook, stirring frequently, until butter is melted and mixture is heated. Remove from heat.

3. Drain potatoes. Add heated buttermilk mixture. Mash with a potato masher until smooth. Stir in horseradish, salt and pepper. Serve immediately.

Nutritional analysis per serving:
246 calories, 16.5 g fat, 3.5 g protein, 22.5 g carbohydrate, 2.2 g fibre, 399 mg sodium

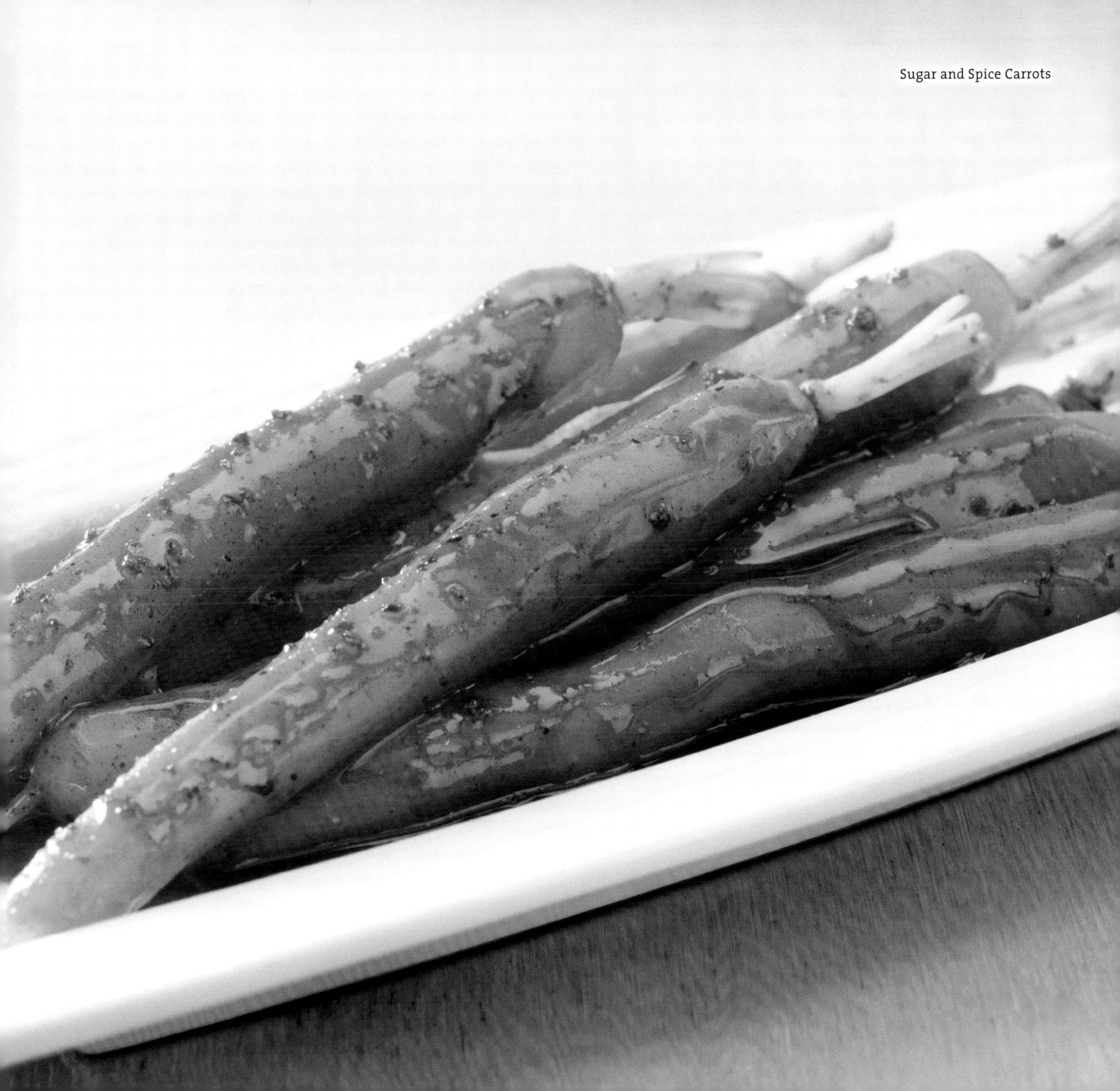

Sugar and Spice Carrots

Spaghetti Squash with Kale Pesto

Ingredients:

1 spaghetti squash (about 2 lb), halved lengthwise and seeded

1 tbsp canola oil

¼ tsp salt

¼ tsp freshly ground pepper

½ cup *Kale Pesto (recipe follows)*

Freshly grated Parmesan cheese*

Serves 6

1. Preheat oven to 400°F.

2. Brush cut sides of squash halves with oil. Sprinkle with salt and pepper.

3. Place squash halves, cut side down, in a parchment paper-lined rimmed baking sheet.

4. Bake, turning squash halves over after 20 minutes, until squash is tender, about 40 minutes.

5. When cool enough to handle, use a fork to pull squash strands free from shell halves; discard shell halves. There should be about 4 cups squash.

6. Transfer squash to a bowl. Add Kale Pesto and toss to combine.

7. Serve topped with Parmesan cheese.

Nutritional analysis per serving:
127 calories, 10.2 g fat, 2.1 g protein, 8.4 g carbohydrate, 2 g fibre, 144 mg sodium

*Ingredient not included in nutritional analysis.

Kale Pesto

Ingredients:

1 cup coarsely chopped kale leaves

¼ cup fresh basil leaves

¼ cup fresh parsley leaves

¼ cup extra-virgin olive oil

3 tbsp slivered almonds, toasted

3 tbsp freshly grated Parmesan cheese

1 tbsp fresh lemon juice

1 clove garlic, chopped

This interesting take on pesto can be enjoyed with pasta or used in our Coddled Eggs with Prosciutto (recipe on page 19).

1. Place all ingredients in a blender; purée until almost smooth. May be refrigerated for up to 3 days or frozen for up to 1 month. Makes about 3/4 cup.

Nutritional analysis per 1 tbsp serving:
58 calories, 5.7 g fat, 1 g protein, 1.3 g carbohydrate, 0.4 g fibre, 22 mg sodium

Spaghetti Squash with Kale Pesto

Ingredients:

3 cups dried navy beans, rinsed and drained

9 cups cold water

2 cups diced bacon

2 cups chopped onions

6 cloves garlic, finely chopped

1 can (28 oz/796 mL) diced tomatoes

3 cups water

½ cup packed dark brown sugar

1 tbsp chili powder

2 tsp dry mustard

2 tsp ground coriander

2 tsp ground cumin

2 tsp smoked paprika

1 tsp salt

2 bay leaves

Serves 12

Pressure Cooker Baked Beans

1. Place beans in a large non-reactive bowl. Pour 9 cups cold water over beans. Cover and refrigerate overnight.

2. Drain beans and set aside.

3. Sauté bacon in a 6 quart pressure cooker over medium heat until browned and crisp. Add onions and garlic; sauté until onions are softened, about 6 minutes.

4. Add soaked beans, tomatoes, 3 cups water, brown sugar, chili powder, dry mustard, coriander, cumin, paprika, salt and bay leaves; stir to combine. Cover with lid and lock it in place. Bring to high pressure over high heat.

5. Cook for 40 minutes, adjusting heat as needed to maintain high pressure.

6. Carefully remove from heat and allow steam to release naturally. This may take 15 – 20 minutes.

7. Wearing oven mitts, carefully open lid away from yourself to protect from steam. Stir baked beans. Remove and discard bay leaves.

Nutritional analysis per serving:
448 calories, 22.7 g fat, 16 g protein, 47 g carbohydrate, 14.3 g fibre, 574 mg sodium

 Cook's Note: Navy beans are also known as small white beans. Dried navy beans can be found in most large grocery stores; they are sold either in bags or in the bulk foods section.

Vanilla Citrus Semifreddo

Sweets, Treats & Other Eats

Ingredients:

4 cups whipping cream

½ cup granulated sugar

¼ cup fresh lemon juice

1 tbsp grated lemon peel

1 tbsp vanilla

1 cup cold homogenized milk

2 envelopes unflavoured gelatin

Serves 16

Did You Know?

Unflavoured gelatin is sold in boxes containing small envelopes of gelatin. One envelope contains 1 tablespoon of gelatin.

 To learn how to make Vanilla Citrus Semifreddo, visit our YouTube channel at youtube.com/TheBlueFlameKitchen

Vanilla Citrus Semifreddo

Semifreddo literally means "half cold". This Italian term is used to describe a cold or partially frozen dessert. Serve slices of this rich and creamy dessert with our Sangria Jelly (recipe on page 91).

1. Combine cream, sugar, lemon juice, lemon peel and vanilla in a large non-reactive saucepan. Bring to a boil over medium heat.

2. Reduce heat and simmer, uncovered, stirring occasionally, for 5 minutes. Remove from heat.

3. Whisk together cold milk and gelatin in a medium heatproof bowl.

4. Gradually stir in hot cream mixture, ½ cup at a time, stirring constantly until combined. Let cool for 5 minutes, stirring occasionally.

5. Pour mixture into a greased 9x5 inch loaf pan lined with plastic wrap that overhangs by 2 inches. Cool to room temperature.

6. Cover and freeze for at least 8 hours or up to 24 hours.

7. To serve, remove pan from freezer. Let stand for 15 minutes.

8. Uncover; using plastic wrap as an aid, lift semifreddo from pan and invert semifreddo onto a cutting board. Remove plastic wrap and slice semifreddo. Serve immediately.

Nutritional analysis per serving:
247 calories, 22.7 g fat, 2.5 g protein, 9.1 g carbohydrate, 0.1 g fibre, 32 mg sodium

 Many natural gas fireplaces will still operate during a power outage. Learn about more of the benefits of using natural gas at atcogas.com.

Sangria Jelly

The colour and flavour of this jelly is reminiscent of sangria, a deep-red drink typically made with red wine and fruit.

1. Place strawberries in a mini food processor; process until smooth.

2. Force strawberry purée through a cheesecloth-lined sieve into a bowl; discard solids. Measure out 1/3 cup strawberry juice; reserve any remaining strawberry juice for another use.

3. Combine 1/3 cup strawberry juice, orange juice, lemon juice, Grand Marnier, orange peel and lemon peel in a non-reactive Dutch oven. Add pectin and stir to combine. Bring to a full rolling boil over high heat, stirring constantly; boil, stirring, for 1 minute.

4. Immediately add sugar and wine; stir to combine. Return to a full rolling boil, stirring constantly; boil hard, stirring, for 1 minute. Remove from heat and skim foam.

5. Ladle jelly into hot sterilized quarter-pint (125 mL) jars, leaving 1/4 inch headspace. Remove air bubbles with a narrow rubber spatula or plastic knife. If necessary, add additional jelly to maintain headspace. Wipe jar rims thoroughly with a clean damp cloth.

6. Seal and process in a boiling water bath for 10 minutes at all altitudes in Alberta.

Nutritional analysis per 1 tbsp serving:
45 calories, 0 g fat, 0 g protein, 10.1 g carbohydrate, 0.1 g fibre, 2 mg sodium

Ingredients:

1 cup quartered strawberries

1/4 cup fresh orange juice

2 tbsp fresh lemon juice

2 tbsp Grand Marnier or other orange liqueur

1 tbsp grated orange peel

1 tbsp grated lemon peel

1 pkg (57 g) Bernardin Original Fruit Pectin Crystals

4 cups granulated sugar

3 cups dry red wine

Makes about 5 1/2 cups

Did You Know?

We have complete preserving information and recipes on our website at atcoblueflamekitchen.com.

Ingredients:

3 cups ice cubes

½ cup fresh mint leaves

¼ cup yuzu juice or fresh lemon juice

12 dashes angostura bitters (about ½ tsp)*

8 cups (2 L) ginger ale

Serves 10

Summer Sipper

This drink is also great with vodka. If desired, stir some in before serving.

1. Layer ice cubes and mint leaves in a large pitcher. Gently stir ice mixture 6 times to bruise mint leaves. Add yuzu juice and bitters; stir to combine. Add ginger ale and stir to combine. Serve immediately.

Nutritional analysis per serving:
69 calories, 0 g fat, 0.1 g protein, 17.9 g carbohydrate, 0.2 g fibre, 16 mg sodium

*Ingredient not included in nutritional analysis.

Cook's Note: A yuzu is a Japanese citrus fruit. Look for yuzu juice in Asian grocery stores.

Angostura bitters were first used as a digestive aid. Today, they are more commonly used for flavouring beverages and foods, and they are also an important ingredient in many cocktails. When added to a beverage or dish, they do not add bitterness but instead act as a flavour enhancer for the other ingredients. Angostura bitters are sold in a small bottle and usually found in the aisle where beverages or carbonated beverages are sold in grocery stores.

Ingredients:

3 cups fresh or frozen raspberries

½ cup water

3 tbsp granulated sugar

2 cups all-purpose flour

2 tsp baking powder

¼ tsp salt

½ cup salted butter, softened

1 cup granulated sugar

2 large eggs

1 tsp vanilla

¼ cup whipping cream

Simple Butter Frosting (recipe follows)

Makes 15

Raspberry Cupcakes

1. Preheat oven to 350°F.

2. To prepare raspberry syrup, combine raspberries, water and 3 tbsp sugar in a small non-reactive saucepan. Bring to a boil.

3. Reduce heat and simmer, uncovered, stirring occasionally, for 10 minutes. Remove from heat.

4. Force mixture through a fine sieve into a heatproof bowl; discard solids. Measure out ¾ cup raspberry syrup and set aside; reserve any remaining raspberry syrup for another use.

5. Combine flour, baking powder and salt in a bowl; set aside.

6. Using medium speed of an electric mixer, beat together butter and 1 cup sugar until fluffy. Beat in eggs, one at a time, beating well after each addition. Beat in vanilla until blended. Combine ¾ cup raspberry syrup and cream.

7. Beginning and ending with flour mixture, add flour mixture alternately with raspberry syrup mixture to butter mixture, beating after each addition until blended. Continue beating until batter is smooth and light, about 2 minutes.

8. Spoon batter into paper-lined muffin cups, filling cups two-thirds full.

9. Bake until a cake tester inserted in centres comes out clean, about 20 – 25 minutes.

10. Cool cupcakes in pans for 5 minutes. Remove from pans and cool completely on racks.

11. Pipe or spread Simple Butter Frosting over tops of cupcakes.

Nutritional analysis per cupcake:
388 calories, 18.4 g fat, 2.9 g protein, 54.2 g carbohydrate, 0.5 g fibre, 235 mg sodium

Ingredients:

¾ cup salted butter, softened

3 cups icing sugar

2 tbsp whipping cream

1 tsp vanilla

Simple Butter Frosting

1. Using medium speed of an electric mixer, beat butter until light and creamy. Gradually beat in icing sugar until combined. Beat in cream and vanilla until fluffy and smooth, about 2 minutes. May be frozen. Makes about 2 cups.

Nutritional analysis per 1 tbsp serving:
86 calories, 4.7 g fat, 0.1 g protein, 11.3 g carbohydrate, 0 g fibre, 39 mg sodium

Raspberry Cupcakes, S'more Cupcakes (page 98)

Ingredients:

1½ lb unpeeled sweet potatoes

Canola oil (for roasting sweet potatoes)*

1 cup whipping cream

3 large eggs, lightly beaten

2 tbsp fancy molasses

½ cup granulated sugar

½ cup packed golden brown sugar

1 tbsp all-purpose flour

½ tsp ground ginger

¼ tsp ground cardamom

¼ tsp ground cloves

¼ tsp nutmeg

¼ tsp salt

Baked *Basic Pie Crust (recipe on page 99)*

Serves 8

Sweet Potato Pie

Even though this unique pie's main ingredient is a vegetable, it makes a delicious dessert. Serve it with whipped cream for a special touch.

1. Preheat oven to 400°F.

2. Combine sweet potatoes and oil in a bowl; toss to coat. Wrap sweet potatoes tightly in foil and place in a baking dish.

3. Bake until tender when pierced with a fork, about 60 – 65 minutes.

4. Unwrap sweet potatoes. When cool enough to handle, peel and mash sweet potatoes. Measure out 2 cups mashed sweet potatoes and cool completely; reserve any remaining mashed sweet potatoes for another use.

5. Preheat oven to 350°F.

6. To prepare filling, whisk together 2 cups mashed sweet potatoes, cream, eggs and molasses in a bowl until blended.

7. Combine sugar, brown sugar, flour, ginger, cardamom, cloves, nutmeg and salt.

8. Add sugar mixture to sweet potato mixture and whisk until smooth.

9. Pour filling into baked Basic Pie Crust.

10. Bake until filling is firm around edges and jiggles just slightly in centre when shaken, about 60 – 70 minutes.

11. Cool pie completely in pie plate on a rack.

12. Refrigerate until serving.

Nutritional analysis per serving:
474 calories, 25.4 g fat, 6.2 g protein, 56.9 g carbohydrate, 2.3 g fibre, 258 mg sodium

*Ingredient not included in nutritional analysis.

 Cook's Note: Any leftover filling may be poured into a heatproof ramekin or custard cup and placed in a small baking pan. Pour enough hot water into pan to come halfway up sides of ramekin. Bake with pie until filling is firm around edges and jiggles just slightly in centre when shaken. Remove ramekin from pan and cool custard completely in ramekin on a rack. Refrigerate until serving.

Sweet Potato Pie

Ingredients:

1 cup all-purpose flour

¾ cup graham wafer crumbs

1 tbsp baking powder

½ tsp salt

½ cup salted butter, softened

½ cup granulated sugar

¼ cup liquid honey

2 large eggs

1 tsp vanilla

¼ cup milk (2%)

Chocolate Marshmallow Filling (recipe on page 99)

4 cups miniature marshmallows

Makes 18

Did You Know?

Baking powder must be fresh to ensure success with baked goods. To check for freshness, combine 1 tsp baking powder and ⅓ cup hot water. This mixture should produce enthusiastic bubbling.

S'more Cupcakes

Reminiscent of s'mores, the campfire treat, these fun cupcakes contain graham wafer crumbs and have a chocolate marshmallow filling with a broiled marshmallow topping.

1. Preheat oven to 350°F.

2. Combine flour, crumbs, baking powder and salt in a bowl; set aside.

3. Using medium speed of an electric mixer, beat together butter, sugar and honey until fluffy. Beat in eggs, one at a time, beating well after each addition. Beat in vanilla until blended.

4. Using low speed, gradually beat in half of flour mixture. Add milk and beat until blended. Gradually beat in remaining flour mixture just until blended.

5. Divide batter among 18 paper-lined muffin cups.

6. Bake until a cake tester inserted in centres comes out clean, about 18 – 20 minutes.

7. Cool cupcakes in pans for 5 minutes.

8. Remove from pans and cool completely on racks.

9. Carefully remove paper liners from cupcakes.

10. Using a cupcake corer or knife and spoon, cut a round hole 1 inch in diameter and 1 inch deep in centre of each cupcake; reserve cupcake centres for another use.

11. Place cupcakes in a rimmed baking sheet. Fill each cupcake hole with about 1 tbsp Chocolate Marshmallow Filling. Arrange about 15 marshmallows over top of each cupcake to cover completely.

12. Preheat broiler.

13. Broil cupcakes until marshmallows are golden brown on top.

Nutritional analysis per cupcake:
245 calories, 9.4 g fat, 2.7 g protein, 38.7 g carbohydrate, 0.7 g fibre, 232 mg sodium

Chocolate Marshmallow Filling

1. Combine marshmallows, milk and butter in a medium saucepan; cook over low heat, stirring frequently, until marshmallows and butter are melted and mixture is smooth. Remove from heat.

2. Add melted chocolate and vanilla; stir until blended.

Nutritional analysis per 1 tbsp serving:
70 calories, 3 g fat, 0.6 g protein, 10.7 g carbohydrate, 0.4 g fibre, 20 mg sodium

Ingredients:

4 cups miniature marshmallows

¼ cup milk (2%)

2 tbsp salted butter

½ cup chopped dark chocolate, melted

1 tsp vanilla

Makes about 1 1/4 cups

Basic Pie Crust

The pastry in this recipe is enough to make a 9 inch single-crust pie crust. The crust is fully baked before it is filled.

1. Combine flour and salt in a bowl. Cut in butter and shortening with a pastry blender until mixture resembles coarse meal. Add ice water, 1 tbsp at a time, mixing lightly with a fork after each addition and adding water just until dough starts to hold together.

2. Gather dough into a ball. Flatten dough into a disc shape. Wrap disc with plastic wrap and refrigerate for 30 minutes before rolling out.

3. Preheat oven to 350°F.

4. Roll out pastry on a lightly floured surface. Fit into a 9 inch pie plate, allowing for ½ inch overhang. Trim, fold and flute edges of pastry. Prick bottom of crust all over with a fork.

5. Line bottom of crust with a piece of parchment paper and fill crust with pie weights, dried beans or raw rice. This helps prevent the crust from shrinking or puffing up during baking.

6. Bake for 30 minutes. Remove pie plate from oven. Remove pie weights and parchment paper.

7. Continue baking for 10 minutes or until crust is fully baked and light golden.

8. Cool crust completely in pie plate on a rack.

Nutritional analysis per ⅛ of recipe:
179 calories, 12.4 g fat, 2.1 g protein, 14.9 g carbohydrate, 0.5 g fibre, 124 mg sodium

Ingredients:

1¼ cups all-purpose flour

¼ tsp salt

¼ cup salted butter, chilled and cubed

¼ cup shortening, chilled and cubed

3 – 5 tbsp ice water

Makes 1 single 9 inch crust

Ingredients:

5 cups bread flour, divided

2 tsp instant yeast

2 tsp salt

1½ cups room temperature water

3 tbsp liquid honey

1 large egg

⅓ cup cream cheese, cut into
  1 inch cubes and softened

Canola oil (for oiling bowl)*

1 large egg yolk

1 tsp water

Makes 2

Did You Know?

Yeast is an ingredient used to leaven baked goods. Instant yeast is mixed directly into a flour mixture as it does not need to be proofed (activated) before using; however, active dry (traditional) yeast needs to be proofed. Active dry yeast is typically proofed by mixing it with warm water or milk and sometimes sugar. This mixture is left to stand until it is foamy, usually about 5 – 10 minutes.

Everyday Bread

This tasty bread is great for sandwiches and toast.

1. Combine 4½ cups flour, yeast and salt in a stand mixer fitted with a flat beater.

2. Add 1½ cups water, honey and egg. Using low speed, beat just until combined.

3. Change stand mixer attachment to a dough hook. Using low speed, gradually beat in cream cheese. If dough is too sticky, beat in remaining ½ cup flour, ¼ cup at a time; continue beating until dough is smooth and elastic, about 8 – 10 minutes.

4. Transfer dough to an oiled bowl; turn dough to coat with oil. Cover with plastic wrap. Let dough rise in a warm draft-free place until doubled in volume, about 1 hour.

5. On a lightly floured surface, divide dough in half. Roll one half of dough into an 8x10 inch rectangle. Starting with a short edge, roll up dough, jelly-roll fashion, forming a loaf. Pinch dough along edge to seal. Repeat procedure with remaining half of dough.

6. Place each loaf, seam side down, in a greased 9x5 inch loaf pan. Cover with greased plastic wrap. Let rise in a warm draft-free place until doubled in volume, about 30 minutes.

7. Meanwhile, preheat oven to 375°F. Whisk together egg yolk and 1 tsp water until blended.

8. Uncover loaves and brush tops with egg yolk mixture.

9. Bake until loaves are golden brown, about 30 – 35 minutes.

10. Cool loaves in pans on racks for 10 minutes.

11. Invert loaves onto racks and cool completely. May be frozen.

Nutritional analysis per ½ inch slice:
86 calories, 1.3 g fat, 2.7 g protein, 15.5 g carbohydrate, 0.5 g fibre, 139 mg sodium

*Ingredient not included in nutritional analysis.

Rye Bread

Ingredients:

3 cups bread flour

1 cup rye flour

2 tsp instant yeast

1½ tsp salt

1 tsp caraway seed

1½ cups warm water (100°F – 110°F)

2 tbsp canola oil

1 tbsp liquid honey

1 large egg

1 tsp water

Makes 1

1. Combine bread flour, rye flour, yeast, salt and caraway seed in a stand mixer fitted with a flat beater.

2. Add 1½ cups warm water, oil and honey. Using low speed, beat just until combined.

3. Change stand mixer attachment to a dough hook. Using low speed, beat until dough is smooth and elastic, about 6 – 8 minutes.

4. Transfer dough to an oiled bowl; turn dough to coat with oil. Cover with plastic wrap. Let dough rise in a warm draft-free place until doubled in volume, about 1¼ – 1½ hours.

5. On a lightly floured surface, roll dough into a 9x14½ inch rectangle. Starting with a long edge, roll up dough, jelly-roll fashion, forming a loaf. Pinch dough along edge to seal.

6. Place loaf, seam side down, in a large parchment paper-lined rimmed baking sheet. Make angled score marks on top of loaf. Cover loosely with greased plastic wrap. Let rise in a warm draft-free place until doubled in volume, about 40 – 60 minutes.

7. Meanwhile, preheat oven to 350°F. Whisk together egg and 1 tsp water until blended.

8. Uncover loaf and brush top with egg mixture.

9. Bake until loaf is golden brown, about 35 – 40 minutes.

10. Remove loaf from pan and cool on a rack. May be frozen.

Nutritional analysis per ½ inch slice:
66 calories, 1.2 g fat, 2.1 g protein, 11.7 g carbohydrate, 0.7 g fibre, 105 mg sodium

 Cook's Note: This dough may be shaped into two smaller loaves. Follow recipe directions, dividing dough in half after first rising and rolling each half into a 5x8 inch rectangle. Leave space between unbaked loaves in pan as loaves will expand during second rising. Loaves should bake in about the same time as one larger loaf.

Rye Bread

Coconut Mango Rice Pudding

Ingredients:

2 cans (400 mL each) coconut milk

½ cup milk (2%)

1 piece lemon grass stalk (6 inch), bruised and chopped

2 tbsp chopped fresh ginger

1 tbsp vanilla

1 tsp grated lime peel

1 tsp salted butter

¾ cup jasmine rice or short grain white rice

1 cup fresh or frozen diced mango

½ cup liquid honey

Serves 5

1. Combine coconut milk, milk, lemon grass, ginger, vanilla and lime peel in a medium non-reactive saucepan. Bring to a simmer over medium heat and cook, uncovered, stirring occasionally, for 5 minutes. Do not boil.

2. Strain coconut milk mixture through a fine sieve into a heatproof bowl; discard solids. Set aside.

3. Melt butter in a medium non-reactive saucepan over low heat. Add rice and sauté until lightly toasted, about 1 – 2 minutes.

4. Add coconut milk mixture and stir to combine. Bring to a simmer over low heat and cook, covered, until rice is tender and mixture is creamy and thickened, about 40 – 45 minutes. Remove from heat.

5. Add mango and honey; stir to combine. Serve warm or cold.

Nutritional analysis per serving:
537 calories, 32.4 g fat, 6 g protein, 61.2 g carbohydrate, 2.6 g fibre, 41 mg sodium

Did You Know?

To use a whole vanilla bean for flavouring a recipe, cut vanilla bean in half lengthwise and scrape beans from pod. Stir beans into ingredients; discard pod.

Blackberry and Rosemary Clafoutis

Clafoutis is a baked dessert of French origin that is made with fruit, usually cherries, and batter.

Ingredients:

⅔ cup milk (2%)

2 large eggs

⅓ cup all-purpose flour

3 tbsp granulated sugar

½ tsp almond extract

⅛ tsp salt

1 cup blackberries

2 tbsp granulated sugar

1 tsp finely chopped fresh rosemary

Whipped cream*

Serves 8

1. Preheat oven to 400°F.

2. To prepare batter, place milk, eggs, flour, 3 tbsp sugar, almond extract and salt in a blender; blend until smooth.

3. Pour batter into a greased 8 inch round baking pan. Place blackberries on top of batter. Sprinkle 2 tbsp sugar and rosemary over batter.

4. Bake until puffed and light golden, about 35 minutes.

5. Let stand for 15 minutes before slicing.

6. Serve warm with a dollop of whipped cream.

Nutritional analysis per serving:
86 calories, 1.7 g fat, 3 g protein, 14.6 g carbohydrate, 1.1 g fibre, 65 mg sodium

*Ingredient not included in nutritional analysis.

Coconut Mango Rice Pudding

Trail Mix

This trail mix makes a great after-school snack and can be taken on the go. Kids and adults alike will enjoy the creative combination.

Ingredients:

2 cups puffed wheat or rice cereal

1 cup unsalted roasted cashews or whole natural almonds

1 cup unsalted blanched roasted peanuts

1 cup sesame sticks

½ cup banana chips

½ cup diced dried mango

½ cup chopped dark chocolate

½ cup peanut butter chips

½ cup sesame seeds

½ cup unsalted shelled pumpkin seeds

½ cup unsweetened shredded coconut

Makes about 8 cups

1. Combine all ingredients in a large bowl.

2. Store in an airtight container in a cool dry place for up to 1 week or freeze for up to 1 month.

Nutritional analysis per ½ cup serving:
277 calories, 20.3 g fat, 8.5 g protein, 17.9 g carbohydrate, 4 g fibre, 37 mg sodium

Blueberry Granola Bars

Ingredients:

7 cups quick-cooking rolled oats, divided

2 cups dried blueberries or raisins

2 cups unsweetened shredded coconut

1 cup wheat germ

½ cup flaxseed

½ cup ground flaxseed

1½ cups salted butter, softened

1½ cups packed golden brown sugar

1 cup liquid honey

1 tbsp vanilla

Makes 40

1. Preheat oven to 325°F.

2. Place 1 cup oats in a mini food processor; process, using an on/off motion, until ground. There should be about 1 cup.

3. Combine ground oats, remaining 6 cups oats, blueberries, coconut, wheat germ, flaxseed and ground flaxseed in a large bowl; set aside.

4. Combine butter, brown sugar, honey and vanilla in a medium saucepan. Bring to a boil over medium heat, stirring frequently. Remove from heat.

5. Pour butter mixture over oats mixture and stir until coated.

6. Using the back of a spoon, firmly press mixture into a greased 12½x17½x1 inch rimmed baking sheet lined with parchment paper that overhangs by 2 inches.

7. Bake until golden brown, about 35 – 40 minutes.

8. Cool completely in pan on a rack. Using parchment paper as an aid, lift granola bar from pan. Cut into bars.

9. Store in an airtight container in refrigerator for up to 4 days. May be frozen.

Nutritional analysis per bar:
261 calories, 12.7 g fat, 3.9 g protein, 34.6 g carbohydrate, 4 g fibre, 68 mg sodium

Trail Mix

Ingredients:

1 whole vanilla bean

2 cups plain Greek yogurt

1½ cups homogenized milk, divided

½ cup liquid honey

2 tbsp grated lemon peel

2 tbsp water

1 envelope unflavoured gelatin

Makes 8

Did You Know?

Greek yogurt is a thick and creamy yogurt. It is made by straining plain yogurt to remove the whey. It is often eaten on its own with granola and fruit, but it is also used in baking and other recipes.

Yogurt Panna Cotta

Panna cotta is a light eggless custard. For a special presentation, serve these with our Sangria Jelly (recipe on page 91).

1. Cut vanilla bean in half lengthwise and reserve half of pod for another use. Scrape beans from remaining half of pod; discard pod.

2. Whisk together beans, yogurt, 1 cup milk, honey and lemon peel in a bowl until blended; set aside.

3. Whisk together water and gelatin in a small heatproof bowl.

4. Heat remaining ½ cup milk in a small saucepan over low heat until steaming and just beginning to simmer. Do not boil. Remove from heat and pour over gelatin mixture; stir until gelatin is dissolved.

5. Add mixture to yogurt mixture and whisk until blended.

6. Divide mixture among eight ¾ cup ramekins or custard cups. Cover and refrigerate until firm or for up to 24 hours.

7. Remove ramekins from refrigerator and uncover.

8. Place one ramekin in a baking pan. Pour enough warm water into pan to come up to level of panna cotta. Let stand for 30 seconds. This helps loosen panna cotta.

9. Remove ramekin from warm water. Run a thin knife around sides of ramekin to loosen. Unmould panna cotta onto an individual dessert plate.

10. Working with one ramekin at a time, place remaining ramekins in warm water in pan and repeat procedure. Serve immediately.

Nutritional analysis per panna cotta:
161 calories, 7 g fat, 4.3 g protein, 22.4 g carbohydrate, 0.2 g fibre, 57 mg sodium

Espresso Cookies

1. Place sugar, brown sugar, espresso granules, cinnamon and salt in a food processor; process to combine.

2. Add egg yolk and process to combine.

3. Add butter and process until mixture is creamy.

4. Add flour, $2/3$ cup at a time, processing after each addition using an on/off motion just until combined.

5. Gather dough into a ball; divide in half. Shape each half into a log 10 inches long.

6. Wrap logs individually in plastic wrap and refrigerate for 1 hour or until firm.

7. Preheat oven to 350°F.

8. Unwrap logs and cut into ¼ inch thick slices.

9. Place slices 1½ inches apart on parchment paper-lined cookie sheets.

10. Bake until edges of cookies are set, about 10 – 12 minutes.

11. Let cookies stand for 5 minutes on cookie sheets.

12. Remove from cookie sheets and cool completely on racks.

13. Transfer cookies to trays. Using a fork, lightly drizzle cookies with melted chocolate. Refrigerate until chocolate is set.

14. Store, layered with parchment paper, in an airtight container in a cool dry place for up to 1 week. May be frozen.

Nutritional analysis per cookie:
54 calories, 3 g fat, 0.5 g protein, 6.4 g carbohydrate, 0.1 g fibre, 43 mg sodium

Ingredients:

½ cup granulated sugar

½ cup packed golden brown sugar

1 tbsp instant espresso coffee granules

½ tsp cinnamon

½ tsp salt

1 large egg yolk

1 cup salted butter, softened

2 cups all-purpose flour

1 oz semi-sweet chocolate, melted

Makes about 5 1/2 dozen

Did You Know?

Espresso is a strong, dark coffee that is served in a small cup. It is also the foundation for many coffee-based beverages, such as cappuccinos and lattes. Espresso is high in caffeine; however, its typical serving size is small so a serving usually has a lower caffeine content than a serving of coffee.

Index